Girl, Don't Count Yourself Out!

You are Resilient, Tenacious, & Faithful

A Compilation By

SABRINA THOMAS

Girl, Don't Count Yourself Out! You are Resilient, Tenacious, & Faithful

Unless otherwise notated, scripture quotations are taken from the Holy Bible, New Living Translation, copyright ©1996, 2004, 2015 by Tyndale House Foundation. Used by permission of Tyndale House Publishers, Carol Stream, Illinois 60188. All rights reserved.

Paperback ISBN: 979-8-218-05280-5

Printed and bound in the United States of America

Book Designed by Brand It Beautifully™

www.branditbeautifully.com

DEDICATION

First, I want to give all the Glory to God. I am blessed to be on this journey God placed on me.

To My Mother, thank you for laying the foundation for me to see what a woman truly is. You have supported me in your own way, and I am so grateful for you.

To My Son Shaquille, I love you to the moon and back. You are my rib. I am so proud of the man you have become.

To My Son Omar, being your mom has changed me for the better and I am so grateful to be on this journey with you.

To My Grandson Kenzo, Gigi loves her suga plum. This legacy I'm building is for you.

To Cordel Cephas, Thank you for all your support in every single way possible.

Contents

Acknowledgments

To Beverly, Natalie, Jolanda, Dr.Daphne, Cathy, Belinda, Star, Latasha, Zontayvia, Kirsha, Rhonda, Julianna and Dr. Karen thank you for sharing your stories to empower women around the world.

To my family and friends who support me and my business. Thanks for your support.

FOREWORD
Dr. Karen L. Maxfield-Lunkin.
#TheWriteRemedyCoach

I had the honor of meeting the amazing visionary author, Sabrina Thomas, four years ago as part of a business cohort /conference in Las Vegas. We later worked together on a book collaboration for Black women bosses. I found her to be focused, friendly, and faith-filled as she pursued her goals while fabulously taking care of her family – mother, children, and grandchild. She has since continued to impress me with her drive and determination to be all that God has called her to be and bring along others with her. I have watched her continue to grow in her resolve to give to and empower her community.

Leading fourteen other women in the writing of this collaboration is a natural next step for Sabrina. Enjoy this literary journey as she encourages others to tell their stories while imparting wisdom, infusing inspiration, and revealing strengths they didn't know they had.

Ms. Thomas embodies the words in this title, which is also an online community. Queen Sabrina is a girlboss and force to be reckoned with in whatever lane she decides to occupy. She is a warm and compassionate leader with a servant's heart. But don't get it twisted –

she leads with the tenacity of a mother eagle, lovingly demanding you get out of that nest and fly!

Girl, Don't Count Yourself Out will challenge you to walk in your God-given purpose and authority in ways you may not be ready for, but still – read on. And whatever you do,

GIRL, DON'T COUNT YOURSELF OUT!

INTRODUCTION
SABRINA THOMAS

Girl, Don't Count Yourself Out is a compilation of the real-life stories of 13 resilient, tenacious and faithful women. These women share stories of how they were able to overcome obstacles that tried to break them. They tell of God's faithfulness in their journey and how they have made it this far.

Challenges are inevitable doses for every single one of us. Even the strongest and smartest of us equally face challenges at different points in our lives. The difference between us is how we respond in the face of these challenges. What do we do when it seems like life is not dancing to the tune of our music? How do we get back on our feet again after falling and having our hearts shattered into a million pieces? Would you rather bury your head in defeat and accept 'your fate' when life throws its ugly side at you? Or would you, like these women, stay strong so you can have a story to tell?

We do not know how strong we can be until we are faced with challenges that test our strength. We really cannot tell what we are capable of until we involve God in our journey. One thing is constant in the stories of these women - they all depended on God. No matter how overwhelming our challenges may seem, we can overcome them with God on our side. So don't you worry anymore! You too, can triumph over your troubles.

These thirteen women share experiences of how they managed to pull through their own challenging times, how they rose above fear, lack of confidence, medical issues, career changes, and domestic relationship situations by drawing strength from God. Having pulled through their tough times, these women have become ministers, advocates, coaches, entrepreneurs, and celebrated world influencers today.

The beautiful thing is that you too, can walk on a path like theirs and still shine forth. Irrespective of what you have experienced, you can come out renewed and strengthened. You also can stand tall above your challenges and refuse to be consumed. Sometimes, all we just need is to be reminded of who we are and the great things we are capable of.

These chapters will remind you that all of us are created with the potential to do whatever we set our minds to. Don't allow obstacles, self-doubt, or anyone to deter you from the path of greatness.

We are all made to bloom, just at different times and in different ways. The trouble is that we are unprepared for challenges, and we often struggle to grasp our own uniqueness. You must believe that God is preparing you for victory and success. With an open heart and willing spirit, let God hold your hand and walk you through your tough times. I am living proof of what prayer, pressing, and holding on to my faith in God will do, can do, has done and is doing! This book will inspire you to trust your journey and remain patient all the way.

As you flip through the pages of this book, prepare yourself to be empowered, inspired, encouraged, and motivated to pull through obstacles and stop counting on yourself. It is going to be a life-changing experience for you as you learn from the stories of women who have walked in the path that you currently walk in. If they could come out triumphantly, you also can. Let no one tell you otherwise.

GIRL, DON'T COUNT YOURSELF OUT!

GIRL, UNLOAD YOUR BAGGAGE
SABRINA THOMAS, VISIONARY, AUTHOR & ADVOCATE

OUR WORLD BECOMES MORE PURPOSEFUL AND BEAUTIFUL when we aspire to the future and the hope it brings. Ten years ago, if anyone had asked me what I'd be doing in ten years' time, I never would have said becoming an author.

Out of the myriad of beautiful things that one could possibly become in life, writing was the very last thing I thought could one day become a reality in my life. But then, you know how life unfolds, plans change, and dreams evolve.

REDEFINING MOMENTS

Sometimes, our life events and occurrences somehow shape our perspectives. They help us find a new purpose and dream. Most of the actions I've taken in the last few years of my life have been birthed in the season of uncertainty and a desperate quest for answers. I was going through a rough patch, trying to figure out my life. Eventually, it led to my rebirth: a period of self-discovery, when I had to face all my fears and find my true strength.

I had to tell myself that it's needless to be afraid or bound by invisible barriers anymore. Then, I had to peel back the layers and do the work. From that point on, I knew it would be a lifelong journey, not necessarily a destination.

However, I struggled and staggered in many battles before I became this newly-discovered (changed) person. I allowed circumstances to weigh me down through the years. But after a while, I realized that I had picked up more than I could accommodate. I had a backpack of limitations strapped to my back that I needed to offload if I was going to unlock my true strength. It dawned on me that if I intended to move toward a new dawn in my life, I had to stop carrying it everywhere. I had to disallow it to be part of my identity.

And I'm convinced that I'm not the only one. Just like me, many other women are suffering the same fate. They are struggling with an invisible backpack filled with judgment, comparison, self-doubt, fear, imposter syndrome, and the need for external validation. As women, we crave that validation badly because it boosts our self-esteem and self-perception.

Working From the Inside Out

Often we evaluate our self-worth based on how we are perceived, appraised, or valued by other people. We indulge the bulk of self-limiting, societal, or trauma-induced beliefs about what we are truly worth. These negative beliefs are there, living rent-free in our heads.

We might not know it, but these are backpacks loaded with everything that keeps us from reaching out for more. These packs keep us down and prevent us from going further to expand and maximize our potential.

Girl, I can relate to your story very well! Why? Because I was once let past circumstances of my life rule and limit my future. My backpack was heavy and laden with pain, fear, self-doubt, and past regrets. Just like you, I wasn't truly living; I merely existed in the shadow of myself. It took the help of God to realize that, in order to grow, excel, and be the woman He created me to be, I needed to open the backpack and clear everything out, one thing after the other. I needed to let everything go!

At one point in my life, I felt stuck and discouraged about my career – so I started my own business years ago. It was at this point I began to realize how I had been holding myself back. I also couldn't figure out how to move out of the funk I was in. But eventually, I did. Through intense coaching, heartfelt prayer, and sincere self-reflection, I was able to identify critical experiences in my life that shaped my self-perception and how I showed up in the world. At last, I was able to connect the dots between what I experienced and how that led to self-doubt. I was finally able to unpack.

So, the time has also come for you to unpack and let go of the weight that continually holds you back from your purpose. The world is here for you to take and conquer.

UNPACK COMPARISON

When you compare your own life with the lives of other people, you unnecessarily set yourself up against them and stir up unhealthy competition. This makes it truly impossible to genuinely celebrate and cheer on other people around you. Why? Because each person's victory is clearly a threat to yours. You can't even celebrate yourself because you're so preoccupied with keeping up with other people's success that you fail to see and celebrate your little wins and victories. Comparing yourself to others will downplay your talents and strength. Remember, we are all different. We've all walked different paths and are all on different journeys and assignments. The only competition you're up against is you.

UNPACK SELF-DOUBT

If you knew how highly God thought of you, you would stop listening to what other people or the voices in your head are whispering to you. God knew what He was doing when He created you. He made you for a unique purpose and particular reasons. Therefore, distance yourself from those who refuse to inspire you to grow and would rather see you brought down. As long as you know your worth and listen to what God says you are, you're on the right path.

KNOW YOUR WORTH

The first step to self-acceptance and belief in yourself is knowing your worth. There's no way you can appreciate the actual value of a thing without knowing its worth. You will never find your worth in someone else in the same way that you will not find your happiness in them either. God has deposited so many beautiful virtues in you.

CONQUER YOUR OWN FEAR

As an individual, fear presents itself in different ways in our lives. However, the effects are mostly similar. The bondage of fear is another thing I had to work on and conquer. Fear is not of God. Anytime you feel scared or anxious, remember that it's the devil trying to penetrate your spirit. God gives His children peace and He wants us to live a joy-filled life.

Remember to be patient with yourself. Life is a journey: we are all growing and evolving differently. Sailing through your journey might not go smoothly, like those routes of other people, but it doesn't mean you won't arrive at your destination. It's okay to have had failures; they don't define you.

UNLOAD IMPOSTER SYNDROME

If you intend to maximize your true potential, imposter syndrome is another item of baggage you'll have to drop. Imposter Syndrome is a feeling of hiding behind a mask of "not belonging" and "not being enough." It can significantly limit your ability to progress in your career, business, and life.

When we step up in any area of life, especially in business, imposter syndrome likes to rear its ugly head. It makes us question our ability to succeed and think we don't deserve it.

All of those old insecurities we thought we'd dealt with start to run through our heads...

"I'm not qualified enough..."

"I'm not experienced enough..."

"I'm not old enough..."

"I'm not pretty enough..."

"I'm not confident enough..."

"I'm not fit enough..."

"I'm not rich enough..."

"I'm not enough..."

Once I figured out where my strengths were and chose to surround myself with people who would encourage me to walk in them, the game changed. My self-awareness became clearer and I could recognize when I was obstructing my own way. Even though I still struggle with imposter syndrome at times, I figure out those triggers that once sent me on a downward spiral while working to increase my confidence in my God-given abilities.

Do the Inner Work

After going through a difficult phase, finding your mental balance isn't simply a walk in the park. However, it is worth it. Building up resilience over time helps you become stronger and wiser. You might not be able to change the past, but you can influence your future. Accept what happened. Process it and take on the lessons. Then, LET GO and move on. Continue to walk in your purpose – after all, some people need you to forgive yourself and get up again so you can help them.

No more complaining. No more excuses. No more fear. No more doubt.

Girl, in this season, your obedience is being accounted for. Your faith is being tested. It is time to level up and make a difference. You are *so* ready. Don't let YOU be the reason you don't do it. Stick to what you know and step out in faith! Girl, Stop Counting Yourself Out. Come on; you can do it.

Resilience:

Life is full of ups and downs. Whether or not we get to our desired zenith depends on whether we remain resilient and resolute in the face of the fiercest storm facing us. We must be determined to triumph amidst life's adversities. It's certain that God will never give you more than you can handle.

God always provides the resources, people, and environments. The question is, will you accept it when the opportunity comes? Will you be sensitive enough to know when He's leading you?

Tenacious:

Be the kind of person who never gives up or stops trying – someone who does whatever is required to accomplish a goal. Sometimes, you will encounter people and events in life that can leave you weary or make you veer off your chosen path. There are situations in life that will break and disappoint you. But you can't quit or run away; instead, trust God and His will for you.

Now is the time you most need your tenacity. Keep pushing to become what God called you to be! Remember, God is always with you. If you pursue your dream with consistency and rugged determination, you will achieve the things you want. And with the power of your faith in God, you will subdue every challenge that comes your way.

FAITHFUL: (HAVING FAITH)

When God isn't providing the answers we desire or moving the mountains we want Him to move, our view of life can become cloudy, shaky, and out of trust. This shakiness then makes us "spiritually frozen," believing that we lack the direction we need to move forward. Faith is produced through perseverance. Instead of sulking and complaining, praise God at all times. Praise Him even when you aren't getting the answers you desire or when no help is in sight. Don't stop doing the inner work and see what God will do.

DON'T COUNT ME OUT

I did the work to transform my life so that I could create a legacy for my sons and grandsons. A life that empowers women to have visible results in their own lives, to awaken their higher self, and to propel them to rise above their situation and become their own hero.

I'm not competing with anyone. I had to really know, understand, and feel that. I decided to start doing the hard things – showing up for myself every day and pushing through! The best thing you can do is allow God to do His job. You cannot worry or fret about any of the things that are already written for your life. In order to move forward, we must let go of everything that's weighing us down.

In the next chapters of this book, you will read the life-changing stories of how 12 other resilient, tenacious, and faithful women unloaded their invisible backpacks and courageously turned their own lives around.

"Don't count me out... I have been built and strengthened by life battles. When you think I'm tired; I am just getting started. When you think I'm dead; that's when I am most alive." – **Steve Maraboli**

GIRL, DON'T COUNT YOURSELF OUT!

ABOUT SABRINA

Sabrina Thomas is an Author, Speaker, Visionary, Publisher, and passionate Autism & Special Education Advocate who empowers parents and caregivers to become their child's best advocates.

Sabrina's first role is as a mother, she has two adult sons, one of whom has an intellectual disability, autism, and cerebral palsy. She has a drive sparked and fueled by her experience as a mother of a son with different abilities. She works with the vision of educating, empowering, and supporting special needs families through her advocacy. With over 20 years of experience as an advocate, she has become a strong voice in her field. Sabrina's mission is to serve as a voice for the special needs community and ensure families never go at it alone and always feel supported.

Hoping to broaden the scope of her work and in line with her vision-- she has started an empowerment community called "Girl Don't Count Yourself Out".

This community aims to connect women from all facets of life to focus on self-care, confidence, and building self-worth. With this movement, Sabrina continues to follow her passion for service by supporting women while they step into becoming the most empowered and uplifted version of themselves.

Today, Sabrina holds certifications in Advocacy, IEP Master Coaching, Speaker Training, as well as a Life Coach certification. Being an established author, Sabrina has co-written 13 books and is an 11-time Amazon Best Seller. In October 2021, she created along with her son but for him, a coloring book series entitled "Color with Omar". These coloring books are a fun learning coloring experience where you get to learn about the creator (Omar) in each series.

Connect with Sabrina

Sabrinatspeaks.com

Facebook and Instagram @girldontcountyourselfout

Healing My Hidden Trauma
Cathy Staton

———

After I was sexually assaulted, I thought my life was over. I thought, "Why me?" I was stripped of my dignity, I had low self-esteem, I didn't love myself, and I didn't know my worth, all because of the trauma I had experienced. I became silent. It would be something that I would not share with anyone because I was afraid. He had threatened to kill me if I said anything. I was silent for years. I felt alone and isolated, so I looked for love in the wrong places. Fast forward: after a failed marriage that involved domestic violence, girl, I had counted myself out!

It wasn't until the age of 41 that I decided I was tired of simply existing and going through life without a purpose. Does this sound like you? My ah-ha moment came when I went into work one day. I was working as a manager for a retail chain, making good money but unhappy and broken. I hated going to work every day. I was starting to get uncomfortable at work and I felt like God was trying to tell me something. I had prayed and prayed before this day for God to give me a sign. I got that sign that day.

I heard a voice, as clear as day, tell me everything was going to be okay. I went to lunch, went to my hotel room, packed my bags, and left. I quit my job of 11 years – and I wasn't worried about a thing because God had told me everything was going to be okay. When I got in my car to drive 10 hours home, I felt like I was having an out of body experience. Nothing looked the same. The clouds seemed so close that I could touch them. As I drove, the bible verse that helped me leave my abusive ex-husband kept coming to me: *"I praise you because I am fearfully and wonderfully made; your works are wonderful; I know that full well"* (Psalm 139:14. NIV).

Something was happening to me. My transformation was taking place. Girl, I went home, cut my hair short, and got a tattoo!!! It was a new me. I had decided that this was the year that I was going to start living, loving myself, and owning my worth. One of the most important things on my mind was the need to start a domestic violence foundation to help women who walked in my shoes. I wanted to use my voice to help those that were afraid to speak out and leave their abusive situations. First, I became a domestic violence speaker and advocate for domestic violence, then I got the courage to share my story about my sexual assault. Sharing my story was pivotal in helping so many women who don't speak up. As a survivor of sexual assault, it was time for me to be honest with myself and the world. I regained control of my life by speaking out against my abusers. I felt that God assigned me to establish a platform for those who are ready to share their stories and to normalize the dialogue for those who remain silent. If you are reading this and are a survivor of sexual assault or domestic violence and are not ready to speak out, I want you to know that it's okay. Speak up and speak out when you're ready.

Getting my life back wasn't easy. Have you ever heard the phrase change your mind, change your life? That's exactly what I had to do. I was determined to create happiness for myself, despite all the struggles I was experiencing. I was also determined to do God's will, not my will. You see, I'd been doing it my way for too long and it wasn't working. How many of you are doing it your way and are tired? Things just aren't working out. You feel stuck and stagnant. I was sick and tired of being sick and tired. It was time to change my life. Don't get me wrong, I still struggle. I pray and meditate daily and I have another go-to bible verse: *"I can do all things through Christ who strengthens me"* (Philippians 4:13, KJV). A lot of people get this verse confused. This verse does not mean that that God will support anything we set out to do or empower us to do whatever impossible things we set our minds to. Paul was telling us that God will give us the confidence to do whatever He calls us to do, not whatever we decide to do.

Want to be set apart? Be authentic. Authenticity implies having a deep understanding of who you are and what you believe in, then expressing yourself openly and consistently to the world. Be yourself. Live apologetically. No one can be you – and that's what sets you apart and makes you different. Your true self is the person you are at the core: someone who doesn't care what other people think of them. In order to have lasting relationships, you must learn how to be your true self. You are authentic when your words, actions, and behaviors consistently reflect your true self.

I'm often told I am resilient. Suffering made me resilient. My suffering included my childhood, sexual assault, domestic violence, and life. In my suffering, God helped me gain the confidence to cope with the stresses of life. When you are resilient, you learn how to maintain control over situations and think of new ways to tackle the problems and stresses of life. The bible tells us *"This too shall pass."* Troubles will come but they won't last. It's the things we go and grow though that matters. Have you bounced back from difficult circumstances? Girl, you're resilient too!!!

I'm living my best life and I know that there's more to come. I want you to know that you can heal from any hidden trauma. There is life after what you went through. There's life after your struggles. Girl, own your worth. You can start doing that by loving yourself. Strengthening your sense of self is key to getting you through successfully and loving yourself. Loving yourself is vital to healing from your hidden trauma.

HERE ARE SOME SUGGESTIONS TO GET YOU ON TRACK TO LOVING YOURSELF MORE AND INCREASING YOUR SELF-WORTH:

1. SERVE THE WORLD BY LIVING YOUR PURPOSE

What is your soul's deepest desire? What is your biggest dream for your own life? Once you find the answers to these questions, you will find your purpose.

2. EMPOWER PEOPLE BY BEING CONFIDENT

It's easier to reduce yourself to a being worthy of compassion. People will feel your misery and will try to help you. On the contrary, however, how inspiring is it to be around somebody who is genuinely confident? It really makes you feel that you can do it too, right?

3. STOP THE GOSSIP, STOP THE COMPLAINTS

Complaining involves a negative energy that locks us into a certain way of thinking. Once we shift our radar towards what in others inspires us, we are instead looking for connection, growth, love, and joy – short, uplifting energies. Those are exactly the qualities we will then be able to nurture in our own lives. It takes time and practice to achieve this shift. The road might be bumpy and you might have to redirect some conversations when you first start practicing. However, it will get easier and easier until it turns from a practice into your second nature!

4. KEEP PROMISES MADE TO YOURSELF

When you make a promise to yourself, KEEP IT! Honor your own word to yourself, whether that be to take a break, go on a holiday, attend a yoga class, eat more healthily, or go to bed early.

5. NOURISH AND CELEBRATE YOURSELF

I've noticed a tendency to discard materialism as something entirely negative. However, I acknowledged to myself how much I love being a girl sometimes, including all those little, pretty things such as make-up, clothes, and spa treatments. Allow yourself to nourish yourself. No matter if that means going to the gym, getting a pedicure, or buying new shoes, do it with a huge smile on your face.

6. HAVE INTEGRITY WITH THE PEOPLE WHO SURROUND YOU

One of my favorite books is The 4 Agreements by Don Miguel Ruiz. The first agreement is, "Be impeccable with your word." There is such depth in this agreement. If we make a promise to ourselves to always be true to ourselves, we start having quality control in the most genuine way. We speak with love. There are certain attitudes and behaviors we don't accept. By doing so, we actually serve humanity. Trust your intuition. Trust your gut.

7. STEP TOWARDS YOUR SOUL'S ALIGNMENT AND DON'T EVER THINK YOU HAVE MORE TIME

Do it now! Take a little step at a time, but don't put it off. Take baby steps in the right direction, even if it's just a little today and a little tomorrow. I'm honored to be walking right there with you!

CONSIDER THIS POWERFUL QUOTE BY MARIANNE WILLIAMSON:

"Our deepest fear is not that we are inadequate. Our deepest fear is that we are powerful beyond measure. It is our light not our darkness that most frightens us. We ask ourselves, who am I to be brilliant, gorgeous, talented and fabulous? Actually, who are you not to be? You are a child of God. You're playing small does not serve the world. There's nothing enlightened about shrinking so that other people won't feel insecure around you. We

were born to make manifest the glory of God that is within us. It's not just in some of us; it's in everyone. And as we let our own light shine, we unconsciously give other people permission to do the same. As we are liberated from our own fear, our presence automatically liberates others."

GIRL, DON'T COUNT YOURSELF OUT!

ABOUT CATHY

Cathy Harris brings with her over 20 years of leadership development experience. Cathy is a five times bestselling author, Navy veteran, Christian counselor, motivational speaker, philanthropist, mental health therapist, and life and business coach. She is the CEO and founder of *My Help My Hope Foundation, Inc.*, a 501c3 nonprofit organization that assists women and children in crisis situations. She is the CEO of Kingdom Coaching & Consulting, LLC., a company that provides affordable life coaching to those who want to reach their maximum potential in life and business.

Cathy is the recipient of many awards and has been featured on many media platforms. The *My Help My Hope Foundation* was selected as a change maker by the Obama administration and Oprah Winfrey in 2017. During her matriculation, Catherine has earned an AS in Psychology, BS in Christian Counseling, BS in Life Coaching, BS in Addiction & Recovery, and a master's degree in Clinical Mental Health Counseling from Liberty University. Cathy currently resides in Virginia and has one adult son.

CONNECT WITH CATHY

thecathystaton.com

Facebook and Instagram @thefireyourfearcoach

Finding Power in My Voice
Latasha Ramsey-Cyprian, Author & Coach

Have you heard of the term imposter syndrome? Well, I struggled with this for way too long, doubting my ability and feeling like a complete fraud. I frequently heard that Black women had to work twice as hard and be twice as smart to get half as far – this was programmed into me at a young age. It was programmed into me to understand that I had to work extra hard to reach success and that handouts were not in my portion. Then there was the "angry Black woman" stereotype, characterizing Black women as bad-tempered, hostile, and overly aggressive. I never wanted to be labeled that way, so I didn't speak up for myself in situations when I should have. I bottled my frustrations when I had every right to express my emotions. That was the onset of my silencing regarding what mattered most. As a result, I became a people-pleaser with an inability to say no. For over two decades, my mindset imprisoned me. I lost my voice, which left me feeling powerless.

Once I started working at 18, I soon realized that, as a woman of color, I was a double minority. I noticed firsthand that rules in the workplace applied to certain people. My voice didn't matter, so I went about my day on eggshells. Proving that I was competent was a never-ending battle. I shared ideas only to have them ignored, but it suddenly made sense when someone of another ethnicity said the same thing. I lost my desire to engage and take part in meetings. Avoiding the stereotype, I remained silent and stayed out of the way so others wouldn't find me aggressive. I sabotaged myself so that others could feel comfortable. I shrunk myself to maintain an image – at the expense of my well-being.

At 21, an opportunity to be a manager presented itself. I was with a different company and looking to grow in my skillset. I was excited about the new position and what came with it, as I knew a pay increase would follow, so I asked the owner about the new pay. He told me it increased twenty-five cents. I knew there was a mistake with the number of responsibilities I had to take on. After expressing my dissatisfaction, the owner told me that was all he could do and, after six months, I would get another raise. Still struggling to use my voice combined with low self-worth, I didn't voice how unacceptable that was. Determined to prove myself again, I accepted the pay. During the six months I went above and beyond, excelling at my job. When others didn't show up, I was there.

Sadly, my pay did not increase as promised. I was invisible to those around me and they repeatedly made sexist comments. It disgusted me to work in such a toxic environment, knowing a pastor owned the company. I could see him front and center with the façade of being a perfect family man outside of work. After reminding him of what he promised, I was gaslighted and told he couldn't afford to pay me more. In my heart, I knew this wasn't the truth, but the way I thought about myself wouldn't allow me to stand up. This man owned several businesses; there was no way he couldn't pay me my worth.

Internally, I'd had enough and immediately started looking for another job. The first job I interviewed with hired me on the spot and offered more money. I was ecstatic and relieved. I gave the owner my two-week notice and he told me I should have talked to him because he didn't know I was unhappy. He tried giving me a raise but, at that point, it was too late. My last day of work fell on my payday. The owner intentionally withheld my pay to control me. I had to see him first to get the paycheck

I'd worked for, but I refused. I would not play into his inflated ego, so I told my father about the situation. My father called the job and told the owner that he needed to give me my paycheck immediately or he would come to my place of work. Within minutes, the owner brought my check to me. I finished my shift and knew I would never return.

Free at last, I started my new job and was happy to be in a new work environment. This time, the owner was a woman. I had a set schedule and was comfortable. I looked forward to the possibilities because of this new role. As with my previous job, I earned a promotion to manager in a short timeframe. I worked extremely hard, as she afforded me the opportunity at five months' gestation and I didn't want my pregnancy to be an excuse for why I couldn't perform my duties. I took on many projects because I didn't know how to say no. Within months, I realized this dynamic was just as emotionally destructive as the previous one. The owner was extremely rude to her employees and, despite my title, she also micromanaged me. Before making a decision, I had to check with her. I didn't want to admit it but she didn't trust me, which bothered me. There I was, a manager who was unable to manage. It was so confusing. It had become a pattern because, once again, I'd tried to prove myself as a competent, intelligent woman. Again, no one saw the value that I brought to the table.

I made up excuses for the owner's behavior at first because I was in denial that someone could be that miserable daily. She would tell me that she was the way she was because employees frequently quit, making her not want to get close to people. Even though she wasn't outright mean to me, I overlooked a lot because my job was the way I supported myself and my daughter.

Months at the company turned into years. It didn't take long to recognize that the owner had underlying issues that resulted in frequent outbursts and rants. There was no room for me to grow and I felt stagnant. The company had an extremely high turnover rate because the owner micromanaged and mistreated staff. The moment an employee would try to explain themselves, she would get upset and fire them on the spot. Once the team left, she would try to justify her toxic behavior. I said little because I knew she wouldn't listen to me. After all, she thought she was always right. I didn't bother trying to get her to see things from my point of view.

I began dreading the job and felt stuck because I didn't have a college degree. There weren't many decent-paying jobs in my town. I spent two hours a day commuting in the car . I lived for Friday and I dreaded Sunday evenings because I didn't want to return to work on Monday. One day, the owner told me that her daughter was about to graduate from college. Congratulating her, I mentioned how I'd thought about going back to finish my degree. She looked at me in disgust and said, "Why would you want to do that at your age?" I knew she didn't care about my loyalty to the company and all I'd sacrificed for her company. It was then I learned that in order to shift, my mindset had to shift first. It was time for me to see the change I desired. I'd had enough of the poor treatment: it was time for me to walk in my purpose and pursue my dreams. I would make no one else rich while downplaying my own abilities.

I immediately enrolled in online night classes and didn't tell anyone outside my immediate family. I created an exit strategy and within 13 months, I got my degree. God blessed me with a job closer to home with benefits and room for growth. The day I put in my two weeks' notice was very liberating. I had been with the company for ten years. My second daughter was five months old and I refused to miss out on the milestones that I'd missed with my first daughter. The owner offered to demote me and pay me less money to stay. She didn't understand that my season there had ended and that offering less money was in no way going to get me to stay. It was evident that she didn't value me.

Once I left that job, I dug deep within and changed how I viewed myself. I'd spent my twenties and half of my thirties not being my authentic self. I had management positions; however, I lacked positional power. I faced issues of diversity on top of inequality. For years, there was an expectation to interact and deal with what everyone had to say, all while keeping a smile on my face. That was unrealistic and unfair. I was misunderstood and undervalued. I experienced daily microaggressions.

I began embracing who I was as a woman and practicing self-love. I humbled myself and got closer to God. He restored my faith and renewed my mindset. God never promised us that life would be easy. I knew I needed strength, endurance, and power to face the challenges I'd put up with for years. Job did not run away from God when he experienced life challenges in the Bible. That story was a glorious reminder for me to keep going. I asked God to take control of my life. I started acting in faith and God blessed me with strength and power – power that I never knew existed. I got my MBA and I started getting certifications in areas that could empower women, such as life coaching and credit restoration. I became more confident in my skillsets, recognizing my worth and talents. Now I empower other marginalized women by letting them know that it's okay to have a voice and talk about inequalities at work to advance personally, financially, and professionally. I encourage the oppressed. After all, when we amplify our voice, we can serve those who go unheard.

We have a voice – and when we speak, people listen. God gives us instruments of influence and we must use these voices to encourage, warn, inspire, and teach. I'm comfortable using my voice now because it is a gift from God that I allowed to be silenced for many years. Our voices are unique and God is creative in how He wants us to use them. As we walk through the doors that He opens for us, we need to communicate the message He gives us at each opportunity. The Most High gives us credibility to speak on issues based on what he's taught us and what we're exposed to. He shows us things for a purpose. Today, I walk entirely in my goals – and I'm committed to doing so for the rest of my life. I found the strength and confidence needed to speak up and be heard. I am no longer silenced.

"Those who trust in the Lord will find new strength. They will soar high on wings like eagles. They will run and not grow weary." - Isaiah 40:31

GIRL, DON'T COUNT YOURSELF OUT!

ABOUT LATASHA

Latasha Ramsey-Cyprian is a native of Abita Springs, LA, and works professionally in HR. Latasha is married and has two daughters, Katelyn and Kyra. She received her MBA from Louisiana State University-Shreveport. Latasha is a two-times bestselling author, credit repair specialist, educator, and certified life coach. Latasha is the owner of Optimum Life Enterprises LLC and Optimum Life Credit Solutions.

As a life coach, Latasha is dedicated to rewiring an individual's mindset and allowing them to be the very best version of themselves. Latasha also provides a credit restoration program.

Latasha is Louisiana state chair for G100 Oneness & Wisdom, board president of Catch My Heart Outreach, member of Hammond-Northshore of Jack & Jill of America, Inc., and member of Tangipahoa Regional Black Business Chamber of Commerce. She is also a member of Tangipahoa Professional Women and a member of International Society of Female Professionals. Latasha focuses heavily on breaking generational curses, women empowerment, and spreading financial literacy.

CONNECT WITH LATASHA

optimumlifecreditsolutions.com

info@optimumlifecreditsolutions.com

What You Gon' Do Baby? Pivots Will Lead to Purpose!

Jolanda "Jo" Logan, Business Consultant & Speaker

Vulnerability isn't something I exhibit often, if ever. And as I considered sharing my story of battling infertility for the first time, I realized that being vulnerable and sharing that story could act as a source of strength, encouragement, and inspiration.

Without question, I get my faith and tenacity from my mother, Noel. She had a quiet demeanor, but her strength and resilience were evident. She had faith, was stoic, and kept moving in spite of everything. And I adopted her way of functioning; I conditioned myself to be the strong one, sometimes to my detriment.

I don't share when I'm going through things. I was taught that it's nobody's business and that you just suck things up and keep moving. Well, I did – until I broke down when confronted with a condition I'd never heard of, a chronic condition with psychological and reproductive manifestations. A disorder that could be the cause of me never becoming a mother.

"You will probably never have children."

Say what? I was only 40 years old, but that was considered 'high risk' when trying to conceive. Being told that I would probably never have children was the last thing I expected.

After the doctor's pronouncement, I felt indescribable pain... I was devastated and ashamed. With this sense of shame I immediately blamed myself. I asked myself "what did I do to cause this?"

It felt like an out of body experience.

Unfortunately, it was real. While I had a desire to be a mom, my body wasn't cooperating in a way that would lead to mine and my husband's dream of being parents coming true.

This revelation caused a myriad of feelings and reactions. While I would typically embrace challenges with an expectant attitude, this time I struggled. Yes, I had dealt with changes that led to me having to 'pivot.' But my feelings of sadness and circumstances so far beyond my control left me paralyzed, with no idea of what to do or what direction to take.

Unbeknownst to me at the time, this series of events would lead to a pivot that resulted in one of my greatest blessings – my son, Christopher Clarence!

SWEET DREAMS ARE MADE OF THIS

Ever since I was a little girl, I dreamed of wearing heels and business suits to my job in a high-rise building! My dream became reality and I was fortunate to work for some of the biggest brands alongside many celebrities.

I met my husband, Christopher, on a blind date in his home state of New York. Set up by my friend and his cousin, I initially rejected the invitation to have dinner with him. Thankfully, I changed my mind and, as they say, the rest is history! When we met, I was working 7 days a week in a high visibility corporate role. I traveled four days out of the week and at least half my day was spent in the office every Saturday. My job was exciting but hectic!

During my corporate career, I was hyper focused, worked 40+ hours including weekends, and did what I thought I had to do to get to the C-suite. But honestly, I was ill-equipped to join the ranks. While I was successful and blessed to be at the table, dealing with constant scrutiny, being overlooked for opportunities, and dealing with microaggressions was stressful, to say the least.

Over time, I no longer enjoyed my job or felt that I was called to make a difference. I knew that I had to make a change when I found myself bawling in the fetal position on my couch, telling my vice president that I was tired of fighting. As a result, I opted to accept a buyout package.

Now, in the midst of all my professional turmoil, my personal life was blossoming! My then-fiancé Chris proposed and we were married in 2007! The pressure was on because errybody was asking "When are you going to have a baby?" I remember calling my parents to share the news that we'd purchased our first home together. Mom and Dad were on the line and when I told them that we had a surprise, Daddy said "You're pregnant!" I said, "Ummm, no, we bought a house!" His immediate response was lackluster but he congratulated us on buying a home. Needless to say, our families were anxiously awaiting a baby.

I automatically assumed that I would be a mom. My little sister is 13 years younger than me and I wasn't just her babysitter but was like her mom! Later in life, when she gave birth, my nephew became my baby by default.

Chris and I had been married four years and we still hadn't been blessed with a child. Meanwhile, friends and family members were giving birth all around me. I felt like a failure. Our baby would be the first child for my husband and I. He or she would also be the first grandchild for my in-laws. Everyone was anxiously awaiting a pregnancy announcement – including me. In the meantime, I felt inadequate and I felt ashamed – ashamed that I couldn't conceive naturally. I didn't share these feelings with anyone, not even my husband. Remember, I had been conditioned to keep things inside. After trying and not seeing a positive pregnancy test result, we decided to see a doctor. It was during a visit to a specialist that I was diagnosed with PCOS – polycystic ovary syndrome.

POLY WHAT?

PCOS is one of the most common causes of female infertility and, according to the Centers for Disease Control and Prevention, affects 6% to 12% (as many as 5 million) of US women of reproductive age.

Having never heard of PCOS prior to diagnosis, I began to educate myself and sought treatment. I recognized that I had experienced some of the symptoms associated with the disorder: difficulty losing weight, thinning hair, and darkening of the skin in body creases and folds. Difficulty conceiving and infertility were the issues that led to my diagnosis.

Women with PCOS have higher levels of androgens (male hormones that females also have), which can stop eggs from being released (ovulation) and cause irregular periods, acne, thinning scalp hair, and excess hair growth on the face and body.

Sadly, Black women are disproportionately affected by polycystic ovary syndrome and many are unaware. It is believed that PCOS is genetic and the chances of having it are greater if other women in your family have PCOS, irregular periods, or diabetes. PCOS can be passed down from either the mother or father's side.

WHAT YOU GON' DO BABY?

My childhood and lifetime best friend's grandmother, Rosetta, was a hardworking and loving but no-nonsense woman. She (and the many women that raised us) would often drop words of wisdom that would serve both Roslyn and I well as adults experiencing the complexities of adulting. I can confidently say that the seeds of the words planted and behaviors modeled would all serve to help me not freak out or quit when times got rough or felt unbearable.

One of Ms. Rosetta's phrases that sticks with me to this day is *"What you gon' do baby?"* Born and raised in Southeast Louisiana, it's common to be called or referred to as baby by anyone! It was Ms.

Rosetta's raised tone and intent expression that made you pay rapt attention when the question was posed.

It's a question that I would ask myself each time I had to navigate the changes and pivots in my life. My battle with infertility was definitely one of those times.

For the many years that I struggled to get pregnant, I would often sit on my closet floor and cry. There were days when the longing for a child was unbearable. Mind you, it seemed that folks around me were getting pregnant right and left... but not me. God, what's wrong with me? What did I do to deserve this? I was wallowing in self-pity and was fire mad at God! And then one day, after a bout of tears and as I nursed the huge headache that came from crying so hard, I asked myself, "***What you gon' do baby?***"

I decided, at that point, it was time for me to do things differently – I needed to pivot. I needed to GET UP, SPEAK LIFE, and DO THE WORK! I could only control my thoughts and actions. The rest was up to God! He promised that He was present to help in times of trouble, so I took Him at His word and trusted Him.

Werk, Werk, Werk, Werk, Werk

First, I PRAYED and processed my feelings of inadequacy and shame. I recalled the story of Hannah and, just as she had done, I petitioned God and asked for a child. I then memorized Samuel 1:27 *"For this child I prayed, and the Lord has granted me my petition which I asked of Him."* I repeated this scripture often as I went through this season. I realized that I didn't need to hide what I was going through, it was okay to cry and talk about my feelings. Chris and I prayed together and we claimed that God would answer our prayers.

Secondly, I researched PCOS and we found a fertility doctor specialized in helping women impacted by the disorder. Dr. P was a divine connection! He was factual and provided sound guidance regarding the process and steps we would take as we attempted to get pregnant. Because of the issues, the doctor felt IVF (in vitro fertilization) would give us the best success rate. IVF is the process of fertilizing the egg with sperm outside of the body. Once fertilized, the embryo is inserted into the uterus.

I must pause here and tell you that the decision to undergo IVF was not made lightly. It's expensive! There are no guarantees and, in addition, IVF entails injections – and your girl don't do needles or anything to do with blood! Nevertheless, I did what I had to do because we believed that this was the answer to our prayers.

Despite my age (40) being considered a big risk factor, two embryos were successfully planted after a few rounds and I was finally pregnant! During the process I battled the side effects of nausea, chronic constipation, emotional issues, and headaches. And we weren't out of the woods yet! While shopping one day, I began spotting and lost an embryo. The fear of miscarrying was paralyzing! I followed the doctor's orders to take it easy and my pregnancy progressed. Fast forward, during a checkup the doctor felt that there might be something wrong with the baby's heart and I had to be monitored weekly. I had to cast down feelings of fear and panic! I talked to the Lord and spoke to my baby. I told him that he was whole, with nothing missing! I told him that he was in good health.

God was with us during every step on this journey! I had a joyful pregnancy and, despite a planned C-section (on my husband's birthday), our son followed God's timing and came naturally three weeks early! Christopher Clarence was beautiful, healthy, and did not cry as he entered the world. His eyes were wide open and he was observing everything around him! His behavior at birth was indicative of what his demeanor would be: he's super intuitive, observant, and extremely intelligent! The child that doctors predicted would never be born is a witty, bilingual honor student with an incredible musical gift. When doctors said no, GOD SAID YES!

Life has thrown you unexpected curves that threw you off balance. You've had to make changes and pivot in a different direction. You are not alone! This story is for those of you who feel like you can't be vulnerable and you can't overcome challenges.

Many curves in my life caused me to pivot – layoffs, infertility, the deaths of my parents, some poor choices, and, honestly, fate! I could have stayed in the depression that I experienced but I chose to embrace my pivots. I recognized that every move in my life, especially my infertility journey, had me on a path – a path to purpose!

So, here's what I learned and what I now apply to every change (pivot) that I face. I pray that you use these steps to help you embrace and leverage your pivots to get to your purpose:

1. **Pause** - Acknowledge that the change or difficulty has happened and feel what you feel (acknowledge and process your emotions)
2. **Prepare** - Consult God for direction and ask Him to help you with any unbelief. Determine what's in your realm of control and make a plan while exercising wisdom. Shift your mindset to 'with God, all things are possible!'
3. **Proceed** - Take action on the things that you can and leave the rest to God! Have faith and continuously speak a positive outcome into existence.

Remember, God is there to ensure that every one of your PIVOTS LEAD TO PURPOSE!

"God is our refuge and strength, a very present help in trouble." - Psalm 46:1

Girl, Don't Count Yourself Out!

Jolanda "Jo" Logan – transformational speaker, business consultant, coach, minister, and strategist – is a reformed 60+ hour a week corporate exec. Her gift is "connecting good people, with good people!" She figures out how information and relationships can be maximized to be mutually beneficial. CEO of Jolanda Logan Consulting, Jolanda helps companies, faith-based organizations, and non-profits develop strategies and execute in the areas of communication, administration, operation, and leadership.

Jolanda's true jam and mission in life is helping others embrace, leverage, and celebrate pivots! She married her Brooklyn-born blind date Christopher and, while she has worked with the likes of R&B legend Patti LaBelle, pop superstar Paula Abdul, gospel great Micah Stampley, and the hip-hop GOAT LL Cool J, she counts their son Christopher Clarence as her biggest achievement and blessing. She's also mom to CJ's fur brother Biscuit, a Yorkie-Bichon Frisé mix who believes that he's a real boy!

Connect with Jolanda

jolandalogan.com

Facebook @JolandaLoganConsulting

Instagram @jolandaloganenterprises

HerToo

Zontayvia Solomon Jiles, MBA & Author

I came into this world alone and I should not be afraid to live it alone, but I have found a weakness of mine: clinging to making everyone else happy.

I am the oldest of four children by my mother. She had me in her teenage years. She quit school to be mother to me. Why? She was so smart in my eyes. Sacrifice! She taught me that sacrifice gives the greatest reward. After a while she sent my sister and I to live with my uncle and family while she ran from an abusive relationship. We had the life that most would have wanted: a nice house, big back yard, nice vehicles... yet something was missing. NORMALITY.

Midway through third grade, my mom came and said we could live with her. I'd never felt so good inside. But boy, was it a culture change. My sister and I were used to going to church three times a week, only listening to gospel, and being in a conservative home. Mom was what we would call "litty." My sister and I had the chance to listen to music that was frowned upon, celebrate the traditional things most kids enjoyed, eat at our own leisure, and had less restrictions. Life was great, I thought.

As time went on, my brother eventually came to live with us. He' lived with our grandmother. My mother had another child. Through these years, my sister and brother would go back and forth between our grandmother and uncle because they missed them. One summer, things changed. Mom said, "I'm tired of you fussing and fighting, you guys will live together and learn to love each other as siblings." From that day forward, we all lived under the same roof until I left for the military. Those days, when I didn't understand, are now reminders of what a mother is and what she must do. My mother taught me that if all else fails, I must continue to be a mother – even when I cannot see anything more. I am obliged to be there for my children. In 2005, I left for Great Lakes Illinois for bootcamp for the United States Navy.

Shortly after enlisting into the military, I was stationed in Jacksonville, Florida. I loved it there. I was free to do whatever I wanted – all I had to do was be at my appointed place on time and do what was asked. That's easy, right? While working I met this guy and thought he was the most handsome man I had ever seen. He had a nice posture and stance, great style, a nice home, and made me feel like I was the most beautiful girl in the world. He was to deploy not long after we met. I instantly thought we shouldn't be together. Once I told him my thoughts, he said, "No, we will whether the storm." We did just that. Once he returned, he proposed and we got married. I was content: it was only he and I.

One day, he decided it was time for a child. He was older, so I understood but refused to change my stance. That was when things shifted. I was determined to complete a degree before having a child. One day my late grandmother asked when I would be giving her a grandchild. I was like, "never, no time soon." She asked about my husband and I told her he was pressing. Granny reminded me that it isn't about that and in order for me to be in a successful marriage, I had to sacrifice a little. I believe I lost myself in that moment, because from then on I felt I had to ensure he was great over myself.

Here comes baby J. He cried the most of any baby I had ever seen. All he did was cry and I hated it. He wouldn't latch so I was forced to pump and bottle feed. One day, one of my friends asked me, "Why do you call your child 'that baby'?" In that moment, he was that baby to me and I didn't understand her reason for asking. As time went on, I learned that I wasn't happy with my child or myself. I didn't want him. I had lost myself. I was miserable. I worked, came home, cooked, cleaned, was mom, and was wife.

My husband's career was taking off – and because his career was taking off, I was reminded that I was a wife and my job was to support him and his endeavors. The key that was missing was that I wasn't caring for myself. I didn't fully understand the meaning of "sacrifice a little." Everything revolved around Baby J and Dad. Dad was so busy with his career he missed the signs of my silent cries. During this time, I enrolled in school to try and gain my wind back. I never quite grabbed it. I was missing promotions by small amounts and I was unhappy at home; I just wanted to ball up in a hole and escape.

The day came when I was forced to make a decision that was beyond my control. I had to leave the military. He didn't seem to care because he was set and could retire – me, on the other hand, I had to figure out my next move. Not once did he help, not once did he care. He was set. I cried many days and nights, wondering if he would ever see me as more than his wife. We would be around people and he would call me "the wife." I felt little, as if I was just something to do or in some position. I made the conscious decision to ask him. He replied that he "heard me" but no action came with it. This hurt me, as I was so supportive of him, his decisions, and his career.

Did he think of me? Did I need a hand? Did I need support? Was my journey not worthy of support? I finally broke. I told him I wasn't happy. He didn't seem to think I was right. His response was that he takes care of home. Home? I am your wife, not home. I asked him to go to counseling. We went, all for him to say that he takes care of his son and me. I still didn't understand. I did everything to make his life easy but he never saw my cries for help. The counselor asked me to schedule a session for myself. Once I begin going to counseling on my own, I began to realize I was lost. All I knew was how to cater to my husband.

Prior to me being released from the military, I rented an apartment and moved out on my own. This was by far one of the hardest things I have ever had to do. I had no idea where to start. I never paid bills because he paid them. I just lived and supported him, he did the rest. After moving into my own place, I found I was a long way from where I needed to be. I moved in the apartment and the lights were on, but guess what? You have to get them switched over. I came home one day to a notice that I needed to come to the leasing office – and there I found out my lights were off. I'd never felt so hurt. There I was with a child and no lights. Was I being selfish for moving out on my own? Should I have just stayed? Do I call him and ask can we stay? With a million questions running through my mind, I made the conscious decision to stay, to wake up the next day, and to take care of business.

Once I was out of the military, I began to gain my wings. I was living on my own, co-parenting, paying my own bills, a reservist, working full-time, and going to college full-time. Look at her go! I was being independent and working on myself. I was doing what I needed to do for me. After a few months, I believe his light went off. We decided we would give love another chance. We moved into my small apartment and decided to work on us. It wasn't about how much he provided but about us being a unit. After the lease was up, we decided on a bigger place – and look at God! Baby J2 was on his way.

Many look at my life and see perfection or don't realize the struggles I've had because I have chosen to continue to fight. I'm here to say that I chose me. Since then, life has been better as I've learned to say, "No! I matter too." I have since completed two degrees and opened my own business. Look at God work. As a child, I never knew what type of family I wanted – I just knew I wanted to be loved and to feel as if I mattered. Now that I'm an adult, I've experienced life a little; it's safe to say that my upbringing taught me more than I thought. There will be storms but you must be intentional with your prayers. God will see you through the storm if you believe in His unwavering love and, most importantly, ask when you don't understand. The conversations that my granny and I shared after my storm were filled with questions. She knew "Mader" had grown to become the woman she knew she could be.

"You have to save yourself, first." – Rudy Silas, Esq

GIRL, DON'T COUNT YOURSELF OUT!

ABOUT ZONTAYVIA

Zontayvia Solomon Jiles is a Georgia native born in Southwest Georgia. She graduated from the town-next-door high school in Moultrie, Georgia, in the same year she joined the United States Navy. She received her associate's degree in Health Care Administration while enlisted in the United States Navy. Upon leaving the military she completed her bachelor's degree and master's degree in Business Management, emphasizing Healthcare Management.

Mrs. Solomon Jiles currently holds the position of a patient safety specialist at a local military treatment facility, a pharmacy technician at a local pharmacy, and the owner of Write Way, LLC, which has expanded beyond her beliefs.

Mrs. Solomon Jiles' ultimate goal is to become a director of medical administration at a hospital. The biggest achievement for her has been beating the odds and being the first in her family to obtain her master's degree and open her own business. Zontayvia enjoys reading, writing, creating, and spending time with family.

Connect with Zontayvia

Instagram @writeway_llc

linktr.ee/writeway_llc

Selected, Shuffled, Shifted, and Solidified

Natalie Purdie

———

Don't be afraid, for I am with you. Don't be discouraged, for I am your God. I will strengthen you and help you. I will hold you up with my victorious right hand. - Isaiah 41:10 NLT

It all started when I was seeking a new job. I was working a temporary job and the assignment was about to end. On this particular day, I decided to venture out to a new career path in hospitality. During my last job I'd traveled a lot and decided I wanted to work at a hotel. I entered the Human Resources department, filled out my application, and the director reviewed it on the spot. She was very impressed and asked me to wait to see if they had any available positions, as the position had just been filled. A few weeks went by and I saw that they were having a job fair. I decided to try again, so I attended the job fair. As my name was called, I could see the director with a look on her face that said it all: "This name is familiar." As I stood up and began to walk toward her, she had a smile on her face and gave a slight chuckle. No, I was not giving up on working at this hotel. I interviewed that day and was selected for a second interview. I was informed that only one position was available and they had narrowed it down to two candidates. The final position would be determined by a typing test. I had been typing since I was in elementary school, when my uncle bought me a typewriter for Christmas. Yet, that didn't mean I would type better than the other candidate. I remember being nervous! The instructions stated, "Type the memo exactly like you see it," which meant I had to back space, tab, indent, etc. The test consisted of accuracy before speed! Often we miss the simplest instructions on a test. I didn't miss it and I was selected!

As I started my new job, I felt the challenge of being the new person. It didn't help that the other candidate was already working there in a different department and everyone hoped she would have gotten my position. Needless to say, everyone wasn't that friendly, but things like that have never deterred me. I found myself trying to figure out a lot on my own and I was too quiet when I should have spoken up. As I approached 30 days, my supervisors called me into a meeting and stated they didn't want to wait 90 days to discuss my work performance. They were very kind and believed in me, but there was some doubt because I wasn't performing at the pace I should have been. They pulled out the training schedule to review what was missing. They prepared this training schedule with the entire department prior to my start date. As they both started to discuss my training, I informed them that I had never seen the schedule and was never trained by anyone. "I was thrown to the wolves!" They were stunned and disappointed that I was being sabotaged to fail. I was clueless! I learned how to work the system by reading, training myself, and trying to mirror what I saw others doing. They went to the director of sales to report what had happened. From that day forward, I was trained correctly by the people who didn't want to train me. I didn't take it personally. I knew that I needed to learn all that I could and to be the best because that was why I was selected. I learned so much that I could answer clients' questions without consulting my supervisors. I mastered my duties and loved my job.

A few years later the hotel was sold, which caused a shuffle. Just like the business definition – "*when investors change the way their investments are organized in order to make as much money as possible*" - that is exactly what happened. The general manager, our benefits, and the entire HR department changed, which meant so did the employee policies. Many jumped ship and suggested I do the same. I was comfortable in my position and other important factors weighed into why I did not leave. The location was close to my childcare and, as a single parent, that was very important. I also had medical, dental, and vision insurance – if I were to take a new job, I would have to factor in switching everything and going without for a few months. I prayed and rode the wave.

The hotel got sold again a year later! So many changes all over again. This time it was like a dance. Those who had been there now knew the steps of the shuffle, but it wasn't like we knew what song would be played – and that made a difference. This time I started interviewing at different places, but none of them seemed to be the best move at the time. Some places were too far, some didn't offer comparable insurance, and many weren't offering enough money for me to provide for my family. The hotel was sold again for the third time and, just like a deck of cards, everything was shuffled. This shuffle was different. Many details of the hotel changed, from department heads to hourly employees and even renovations. The only thing that didn't change was the name. Like a rollercoaster I gripped on tight, closed my eyes, and prayed hard. I even started a bad habit – smoking cigarettes – to try and ease the stress.

With these new changes, I was transferred to another department. Instead of being discouraged, I told myself that it wasn't a bad thing. I wasn't fired. Others hoped I would give up during this transition but that was something I couldn't do. I told myself that even though I was now shifted, I would learn everything I could in the new department because that would be my weapon. Knowledge is power! I embraced my new role and found that, in this department, everyone was willing to share their knowledge and help!

Then one day, just as I was feeling positive and upbeat, I was crushed. I was informed that I needed to wear a uniform. I would only receive two shirts, a blazer, a skirt, and a pair of pants. My mother always taught me to dress for success and to look like the position you want, not the one that you may be in. I always made sure that my attire was that of an executive. This wardrobe change meant I'd have to spend more money on laundry and all of the clothes I'd purchased for work would be a waste. I wanted to leave. I was livid and overwhelmed with the biased treatment. No one else had to wear a uniform. How could I fight this battle? I prayed and remembered that I didn't always have a huge wardrobe. When you only have a few items, you have to make the best of it: you need to make it look like you have more than you do. I kept with the white shirt requirement but put a twist on it and wore classic tailored shirts with French cuffs. I added my monogrammed cuff links. I made sure my shoes were always stylish to make it look like I wore the suit on purpose, not just because it was a basic uniform. Nevertheless, despite the battle of the wardrobe policy, I would not allow myself to be counted out.

My hard work and perseverance were solidified and I was promoted. With my promotion, I received my own office and no longer had to wear a uniform. I was doing great in my new role. I saw myself there for many years to come. I had built a strong clientele of repeat business. Every morning on my way to work, I would take the opportunity to pray the same prayer as I approached the building. I prayed, "God, please have your Angels build a hedge of protection around me, give me favor amongst my employers, employees, and clients."

One day I came into work on time with everyone else. Usually I would always arrive early, being the first person in and the last to leave. This particular day it was my youngest son's birthday and I had just moved into a new house the night before, which was further away. My day seemed off kilter. I noticed that my lead director had his door closed all day, which he never did. I was working so hard that day that I missed lunch. I then learned that the executives from our corporate office were in the building. I saw a director from another department and she looked bothered. I assumed she was stressed due to the demands of a new executive team, so I tried to encourage her. She was clearly upset and abruptly walked away. As I returned to my office, I was summoned into my lead director's office and, when I entered, there sat the general manager with a file. My heart sank. I knew that I was a hard worker but I knew it couldn't be good to see them there.

They both spoke but I couldn't hear anything they said. I was being laid off. My world was crushed. I'd put the job before my children and never worked less than 10 hours a day for the 9 years I was there. All I could think was "Why me?" I left the building and I got sick. I didn't want anyone to see me vomiting. The director that I'd tried to encourage and another co-worker found me. It all made since why they'd seemed to act strangely and why the director was upset – they knew and were stuck between a rock and a hard place. They couldn't tell me! I didn't know how I would celebrate my son when I was devastated. And what about the new house?

My career had started the day I attended that job fair. However, I had no clue about the road that would be traveled. This seemed like it would be the time for me to count myself out, but it was just a part of being solidified. I forgot about the prayer just that fast – the prayer I'd prayed for so long, every day. The file that the general manager held had contained paychecks for my severance pay, sick leave, and my final paycheck, which was a blessing in that at least I wouldn't have to wait for our pay day. The company had decided to lay off several people a week before, which included the last ones that had been promoted. All part of the shuffle. So even though I had been there longer than many, I had just gotten a promotion. Another act of God's favor was that the general manager delayed the termination until the 1st, so I had all of my medical coverage for 30 days. As a result of me working so much, I had neglected taking my children for their check-ups. This gave me more time. In addition, the director called around to other hotels and recommended that they hire me. The general manager also offered me a letter of recommendation. In fact, I went on to succeed even more in my career and made the next hotel over $1.23 million dollars in sales in one year! Girl, don't count yourself out, even when others do!

"Go where your effort is appreciated. Don't let your actions go unnoticed by individuals who are never satisfied." - Billy Chapata

GIRL, DON'T COUNT YOURSELF OUT!

ABOUT NATALIE

Natalie Purdie is a domestic violence advocate, expert, and speaker of domestic violence, human trafficking, and sexual assault. Natalie's story of how she survived intimate partner violence has touched the lives of millions around the world and possibly prevented other cases of domestic violence. She has spoken out vigilantly about her experience via numerous speaking engagements, training platforms, and media outlets including WATC TV 57, Investigation Discovery [ID] Channel, Lifetime Movie Network, The Real Housewives of Atlanta, and Dr. Oz. Natalie is a board member and volunteer with My Help My Hope Foundation, Inc.

Natalie is teaching a Teen Dating Violence Prevention Program for middle and high school students. Natalie is also on the GA Human Trafficking Task Force with the Criminal Justice Coordinating Council. Natalie helps victims become survivors and works with families who are seeking help for their loved ones.

Connect with Natalie

Nataliepurdie@yahoo.com

Facebook @NataliePurdieSV

Instagram @Survivors_voice

DIVINE ALIGNMENT
BEVERLY ROWDEN, LMSW

———

It was June of 2014 when I arrived at the George Allen Courts Building in Dallas, Texas, for my divorce hearing. Nervous, ambivalent, and downright fearful, I walked into that courtroom with the look of a confident woman – though inwardly, I was anything but. Fearful of the court proceedings? No. Fearful about my future? Yes! Many of those worrisome but realistic thoughts suddenly began to flood my mind and demand my attention. Thoughts about taking care of my autistic son, thoughts about my future as a single woman, financial concerns, and on and on. My thoughts were racing faster than I could process them, causing my anxiety thermometer to reach an all-time high.

The rain was unrelenting and the clouds matched the dreariness of my emotions. "Lord, help me get through this day," I asked as I sat waiting for my name to be called. "Excuse me?" asked the lady sitting next to me. "Oh, I'm sorry, I was just talking to myself," I explained. "I do that a lot too," said this cheery-looking stranger as we both shared a muffled laugh. And just like that, my anxiety thermometer began to decrease. "Thank you, Lord," I said, though this time quietly. After the five-minute hearing was over, I walked briskly out of that old courthouse with my former name and a fresh start. Although my emotions were jumbled, I felt a peace I hadn't felt before. An under-girding peace that, according to Philippians 4:7, is "the peace of God, which surpasses all understanding..."

The rain had stopped, yet the clouds joined forces to keep the sun at bay. While driving home, I witnessed the sun continuously trying to peek through the heaviness of the clouds as if determined to break forth. Before the day was over, its efforts proved successful and could not be ignored. I, too, was determined: determined to overcome and conquer fear, inadequacy, and despondency. I needed to look to Him who overcame so that I might overcome. Romans 8:37 reminded me that I am more than a conqueror, through Him who loved me. *This is my pathway of discovery and finding peace with my new normal.*

HEALING

I am a fierce protector of my privacy and have never been one to openly discuss personal areas of my life, including my divorce, with anyone. However, God was directing my path towards routes of healing that were quite uncomfortable for me. Our church has a ministry called "free at last," which provides support groups led by trained facilitators and counselors for anyone needing to experience freedom from various addictions, unhealthy boundaries, grief, divorce, and more. I knew I was being led to register for the next divorce-care session. I buckled and gave way to shame and doubt. However, since the uneasiness I felt in my spirit refused to subside, I reluctantly registered for the next session. But God knew exactly where I needed to be during this phase of healing and the wealth of information and support I received from this eight-week group session was invaluable. Many of the questions I had about my fluctuating emotions were explained and it was comforting to listen to others share their journeys to wholeness after divorce.

My Saturday morning prayer team became another source of support that God connected me with while traveling down the pathway to healing and wholeness. God used these "seasoned saints" to provide comfort and encouragement to me during this season of evolution. I would also be remiss if I failed to mention the ongoing support of my beautiful children, family, and faithful friends.

Healing from a twenty-three-year marriage could not be hastened, as I soon learned. I tried rushing through this process and checking it off, as if it were a task on my to-do list. However, healing takes time and I eventually accepted the fact that I needed to be patient with myself. I've often heard the expression that *"time* heals all." I choose to believe that *God* heals in time – and only after you have allowed Him to place His healing balm on your open wound. I couldn't pretend and mask my feelings with the all-knowing, omniscient God. I had to be open and honest about my mental and emotional status if I wanted to experience the healing that only He could give. *"For He knows the secrets of the heart"* (Ps. 44:21).

There were many days when peace eluded me and anxiety reigned. Satan, the enemy, wanted me to doubt God's word and walk by sight instead of by faith. Instead, I would renew my mind and counteract Satan's lies with the truth of God's word. Regardless of how I felt or how real the issue was, I would choose faith over feelings and believe what God said, referencing scriptures to speak to whatever distress I was experiencing at the time. Scriptures that I had read countless times now had a deeper, more personal meaning to me. For example, I no longer felt alone in caring for my autistic son as a single parent because the Lord assured me that "never will I leave you, never will I forsake you," Hebrews 13:5. How comforting it is to know that the King of kings and Lord of lords is concerned about that which concerns me. God's word in Philippians 4:6 says that I should be "anxious for nothing ... and to let my requests be made known." God has more than proven Himself faithful during life after divorce. He has made a way out of no way countless times, allowing me to bring glory to His name by sharing my testimonies with others.

Adjusting to my new status included reestablishing myself and becoming grounded as a single woman, which required a great deal of discipline and brought about its own set of challenges. Scheduling, budgeting, decision making, and learning to function in this new role were overwhelming at times, especially during the first year after my divorce. Since stress was intent on becoming my frequent visitor, I had to find a balance and explore different, more meaningful ways to embrace this beautiful life that God had gifted me. So, in the fall of 2016, God placed in my heart the desire to start an autism parent support group in my community, aiming to provide resources, encouragement, and social support to parents and caregivers with common experiences. Living a life of purpose brings glory to the Lord, benefits others, and does a soul good!

SERVING

As time passed and my relationship with the Lord strengthened, fear, inadequacy, and despondency were replaced with courage, confidence, and hope. My test had become my testimony and it wasn't long before I was asked to facilitate a divorce care group. Yes! God was using me to comfort others with the comfort I'd received from Him, as stated in 2 Corinthians 1:4. There is purpose in trials; I was steadfast in growing through them and not just going through them. Sharing my testimony of how God took a broken, fearful, and despondent woman and transformed her into a vessel of hope for others is nothing short of amazing. His grace is utterly amazing!

REJOICING

Ecclesiastes 3:1 states, *"To everything there is a season, A time for every purpose under heaven"* and in verse 4, there's "A time to weep, And a time to laugh; A time to mourn, And a time to dance." I give God a hallelujah praise because my time of laughing and dancing has come. I am enjoying a hope-filled life with new friendships, opportunities, and discoveries. Although rain and cloudy days will continue in the forecast of life, my faith-walk has taught me how to weather the storm without fear, because my savior and deliverer controls the winds and waves. God wants to heal you everywhere you hurt, but you must trust and allow Him into your innermost being with full transparency. If you are angry, afraid, ashamed, or worried, share your feelings with Jehovah Rapha, the

Lord who heals, as He already knows. In fact, according to Luke 12:7, the very hairs of your head are all numbered. That is how intimately the all-loving God knows you!

God wants to give you beauty in exchange for your ashes and bring you through your divorce victoriously. He knows you better than you know yourself and has the best plan for your life. You do not have to settle for less than you deserve or resort to a life of mediocrity. Allow the healing to take place, seek out counseling and/or a support group if you must, and grieve the loss. However, you must refuse to give up on living your best life, because that abundant life awaits you. Jesus thinks so and so should you. God is not a respecter of persons, states Acts 10:34. The same God who brought me through the years, tears, and fears will not withhold His healing and multitude of blessings from you!

God wants to do a new thing in your life. However, if you are content to reflect in the rearview mirror, you will miss what's yet to come. Choose to live purposely and enthusiastically, with a *victor* mindset instead of a *victim* mindset. Resist the urge to throw yourself a pity party; there is nothing to be gained by feeling sorry for yourself. In the words of Joyce Meyer, "You can be pitiful, or you can be powerful, but you can't be both." I made the decision to be powerful with God's strength and I hope you will do the same. Having a "can-do" attitude is a must if you're intent on overcoming the inevitable trials of life. Believe in yourself, practice self-care, and give yourself grace because healing takes time. Most importantly, receive your daily nourishment and spiritual sustenance from the Almighty God through prayer and His word. Just like the sun breaking forth through the clouds, you, too, will break forth with a new-found joy, peace, and confidence from the Son as you discover a new you!

"Fear not, for I am with you, Be not dismayed, for I am your God. I will strengthen you, Yes, I will help you, I will uphold you with My righteous right hand"-Isaiah 41:10.

GIRL, DON'T COUNT YOURSELF OUT!

ABOUT BEVERLY

Beverly D. Rowden, LMSW, began her journey as an assiduous advocate after her son, Dean, was diagnosed with autism at the age of four. Beverly is also the mother of Dr. Ashley Rowden-Schaub, another autism advocate.

Beverly is the founder and president of "Connected Autism Parent Support Foundation", a non-profit organization that provides educational, financial, and social support to parents and caregivers of children and adults on the autism spectrum.

In her efforts to establish more inclusiveness, Beverly's mission is to equip the autism community with knowledge, resources, and support, as she believes everyone has the right to live to their fullest potential.

Beverly received her bachelor's degree in Sociology from Paul Quinn College and her master's degree in Social Work from the University of Texas at Arlington. Beverly is a native Arkansan who has resided in Dallas, Texas, for over thirty years.

CONNECT WITH BEVERLY

beverlyrowdeng@gmail.com

Facebook and Instagram @beverlyrowden9

LIVING BY GRACE
RHONDA PARKER, M.ED & PRESIDENT

GROWING UP IN A SMALL TOWN CALLED SAND BRANCH, Texas, I was fortunate and blessed to be surrounded by family, friends, and extended family who showed me unconditional love and acceptance. I was a shy child who had a love for reading and learning. I spent my days indoors and outdoors, only allowed to play with a select few of friends. Today, I am still able to say that my friendships still exists because of the love and support we gave each other as we allowed ourselves to grow individually and navigate this thing called life.

I had always dreamed of going off to Howard University or a college outside of Texas. Finances didn't allow that to take place. However, I was able to accomplish my goal and attend North Texas State University (or University of North Texas, as it's currently named). I was so excited and nervous because realizing my dream as a first-generation college student had come true. I had always dreamed of going to college because of my love for learning and wanting to be successful. My goal was to be an executive assistant. I was the student that always followed the rules. I even went to school on senior skip day because it was never important to me to follow a crowd. I've always been someone that felt it was important for you to be happy with yourself. Upon entering college, the first in the family to attend a traditional college, my goal was to make my family proud. I realized over time, what does proud mean? I can remember to this day walking onto campus, entering the classroom, and saying to myself "WOOOW." I finally made it, thinking that being in college was going to magically help me achieve all my goals.

Reality hit and I learned how to navigate to being a young adult. Everyone has this idea that when you turn 18, you suddenly understand life. However, the reality is that you're developing into becoming the adult you hope to be one day. The timeframe varies with each individual because everyone has different life experiences.

I didn't understand this at the time. During my time in my undergraduate, I had the opportunity to meet some amazing people, build new friendships, work, and explore my life. I almost joined the air-force due to my love of planes and travel. However, fear once again overtook me because I listen to the voices of others instead of my own. I had this vision of me working in technology and traveling the world. I didn't realize how fear and self-doubt can hold you back from so many life experiences. Sometimes it serves to protect you and other times hinder you, based on how you see it. I didn't see it as a hinderance until much later. Life continued and I changed majors. I was sitting in a business class during my sophomore year and immediately became dissatisfied. I no longer enjoyed the classes. My thoughts were, "I would like to make great money." However, I wanted to have satisfaction in my career. I became involved in the Office of Disabilities by reading for the blind and volunteering my time. My time volunteering, working, and interning during my college years helped me realize the importance of being of service and support to others. I graduated with my Bachelor of Science in Rehabilitation Studies with an emphasis in psychology and sociology.

EARLY ADULT YEARS:

I've been fortunate to be able to work in both the for-profit and non-profit sectors. One of the most amazing experiences that I had was working as an employment consultant for individuals with disabilities. My role was to provide job development, training, research, and any duties that would enable individuals to become employed in their communities. The amazing part is that I had the wonderful opportunity to work with a dedicated staff and amazing people who had many times never held a job. They had been in sheltered workshops or state homes and never had a real opportunity to learn the skills required to obtain a job. My joy came from arriving at my job each day and the clients taking pride in working with me. I was pregnant with my daughter and they would always say, "Don't you work too hard because you have a baby to take care of?" I was so appreciative of them because they were truly more concerned about me. The clients hosted a baby shower for me and one of them had even crotched a special baby blanket. As an employment consultant, I built relationships with organizations such as Fossil, Wendy's, and Olive Garden. I now have the ability to build a watch, which gave me insight into how I was able to adapt in different environments. This opportunity was instrumental in my love for helping others, which was something I truly enjoyed. One of my clients was named Rosita. I trained her for her first job at the age of 50. She ended up having two part-time jobs and did volunteer work alongside that. I only left the job due to the pay at that time in my life.

Passion vs Career

I moved on in my career and have had amazing work experiences with AT&T, Dr. Pepper, WFAA Channel 8 News, The Adolphus Hotel, and back into the nonprofit world working at Nexus Recovery providing vocational services for women in recovery. Once again, the main thread in the positions I held was the opportunity to be of service and support. I have always valued my role in helping others. My time at Nexus Recovery Services was the biggest transition for me because I met this amazing teacher on the campus. She worked for the school district and would teach the students who lived there. I would watch how she interacted with the students and loved how she made connections with them. I enjoyed working with the clients but decided to go into the teaching field.

I jumped in with excitement. I started as a substitute elementary teacher and moved to the high school level. I was accepted immediately into the Alternative Certification Program. I had a plan, as always, but then life happens. I had been hired as a second grade teacher. My goal was always to work in special education but I was placed in the general education setting. I went with the flow, thinking, "Okay, over time my intent is to transition."

Unfortunately, it took a little longer than I expected. After being accepted into the Alternative Certification program, I had started my first full year as a second grade teacher. One day, I woke up and was unable to swallow. I didn't know why but I gradually began to lose weight. I lost over 40 pounds and was unable to lie down to sleep. My doctor had done several tests and referred me to a specialist because they didn't know what was wrong. I literally had to sleep sitting up because I would choke on my saliva if I laid down. I share this because life can change in just one instance. I was fortunate to find a specialist who realized my esophagus was closing, so they had to go in and expand it.

Remember, I was in my first year of teaching in my second grade class. I would come to school weak because I couldn't eat. Imagine the fear in their eyes, wondering what was wrong with the teacher because I was having to miss so much school. I chose to leave the classroom to heal my body. I loved those students but I couldn't be at my best during this time. I did heal and returned to the classroom, but I started in a new district as a special education teacher.

My new position was working at a school for students with behavioral challenges with disabilities. The environment was amazing and they had dedicated teachers and staff. I had a wonderful administrator, Mr. Maurice Walker, because he was professional and compassionate. He truly cared about the students and staff members. I had the opportunity to receive extensive training to support and work with students with autism, disabilities, and behavioral concerns. My first year had over 161 hours of professional training, not including me going to school in the evening to obtain my certification. It was very important to me that I helped my student achieve academic and personal progress in their lives. I received my Special Education Certification within that first year of school. I found so much joy and excitement when one student could say his first word, sentence, or communicate his needs. I know we worked on his communication, academic, and life skills every day, weekend, and holiday. I was also his bus monitor at one time. He showed so much independence in the two years I worked with him and we became actively engaged in attending community-based activities, classes, and events. I can say that it's nothing like working in a classroom. The ability to adapt, work to meet different student needs, parent involvement, school systems, etc. is very challenging and rewarding. I love teaching, training, and mentoring fellow educators. Teaching children and adults comes from the "heart." I can still walk into a classroom of students and feel excited about teaching and learning.

In the past few years I've focused on finding my voice. While I have focused a great deal of my life helping others, which is very important to me, I realized my voice is not only about helping others. It's also about my desire to live while fulfilled in my personal and professional life. I am fortunate enough to truly be in a space where my freedom is not based on money, my career, or people.

Freedom comes from knowing that I was created to fulfill my God-given purpose. I have experienced many challenges personally and professionally, but I refuse to allow my past experiences to define me. I'm on the road to new self-discovery and have stopped allowing my story to be told but instead invite individuals along the journey. I have returned to complete my doctorate (personal goal), develop new programs, travel, build friendships, and develop opportunities that are rewarding and real. I prefer to focus on my purpose filled with faith, family, and friendships sprinkled with grace, joy, and laughter.

But the fruit of the Spirit (the result of His presence within us) is love [unselfish concern for others], joy [inner] peace, patience [not the ability to wait but how we act while waiting], kindness, goodness, faithfulness. - Galatians 5:22 Amplified

GIRL, DON'T COUNT YOURSELF OUT!

ABOUT RHONDA

Ms. Rhonda Parker is certified as an EC-12 educator and rehabilitation counselor, currently a doctoral candidate (2023) in Organizational Leadership, and holds a master's degree in Special Education and a BS in Rehabilitation Studies (emphasis on psychology and sociology). She received a Resolution from the State of Texas as an Outstanding Contributor to Education for the Dallas Independent School District. Rhonda completed a Fellowship with the Department of Education.

Subsequently, Ms. Parker took on the role of founder and executive director of Parker Autism Center (PAC), a 501 © 3 nonprofit dedicated to addressing the needs of individuals and families impacted by autism and multiple disabilities. She has founded Baking To ImPACt and Parker Transition Academy. Rhonda serves and supports students by providing vocational training and community based programming for individuals aged 13 and beyond. She offers organizational training, professional development, and parental support to community members.

When You Have Already Counted Yourself Out

Kirsha Campbell

I READ THE EMAIL AND QUICKLY CLOSED IT. IT COULDN'T BE true. Then I quickly read it again to be sure. Was it a mistake, was it really true? Was it for me? I took a few days before I responded.

The cycle of thinking I would not achieve was one in which I quickly got trapped. Disappointments I experienced didn't make it any better. I remember thinking things would never change in my life. I wouldn't pass my exams, get a better job, get speaking engagements, be a good mom, or even increase my clients.

I'm sure you can relate to moments like this in your life, just expecting things to never get better or even seeing where goals you set weren't realized. Even worse is when you fall off track. It could be a diet you messed up or a bad habit you just can't break! Have you set your schedule and then realized you don't keep up with it or get off track easily?

Now back to the email. It was from a company requesting my services. Why did I think it was a mistake? I didn't believe things would turn around for me. I also didn't think I was worthy.

It sounds pretty cliché... however, it's a sad truth that so many struggle with today. I'm sure you have at some point as well.

WHY ARE YOU ALREADY COUNTING YOURSELF OUT?

Why are you counting yourself out as a mom, woman, corporate professional, entrepreneur, homemaker, student, business owner, volunteer?...Counting out yourself of whatever hat you wear!

Do you...

Think you aren't smart?

Believe you can't offer value?

Doubt your experience?

Think you can't speak well enough?

Think you aren't funny?

Think you've made too many mistakes?

Think you keep messing up?

Think you keep falling short?

Think you'll never bring that task to completion?

The list is endless – and those are all my reasons for counting myself out before. There are still times when I do and I have to be intentional and mindful about not doing that. I say that to you as well, my friend... be intentional and mindful about the awesome things you have to offer.

A part of my culture involved not being confident and subscribing to the lies that I'm not worthy of success or good things. It is one of the biggest lies that impacted my life in a powerful way for years. The remnants still exist and I have to be on the lookout for those moments that subtly creep up – and you should as well!

I am an immigrant. My cultural footprints showed up in a bold way when I relocated. I was afraid to speak or even accept positions that required my expertise. I remember being asked to serve on a board of the Chamber of Commerce and being so afraid... Why? I was afraid to speak and doubted myself in so many ways.

I had to dig deep and remember that God has not given me fear but love, power, and a sound mind. You should too. Fear is a natural emotion. However, fear should not cripple you or your actions. Accept that you're afraid and then decide on the next step. My perspective has continued to change in so many ways. I realized I'd counted myself out in so many ways already and it was a slippery slope to keep doing so. Have you counted yourself out of jobs, relationships, or goals that you set? The list is endless for sure.

How Do You Know if You Have Already Counted Yourself Out?

For I do not do the good I want to do – Romans 7:19 NIV

Have you ever been afraid to apply for an opportunity?

Have you imagined your life differently and thought it can never happen?

Have you perhaps made steps to change your life or habit, then slipped back into old habits or just aborted your goals?

Do you even feel you've failed as a mom? Maybe snapped at your babies too many times or just fell short in various ways and you keep regretting it?

Do you think you may never pass that exam or achieve your goals?

Do you keep looking at the many failures you've had or even disappointing times?

These, my friend, are some instances that may indicate you've already counted yourself out. These instances can become a way of life for you.

You become so used to those thought patterns or actions that you accept them as normal in your life and don't take steps to change. These actions can influence those around you – your children, friends, or other family members and even other relationships, personal or professional. They impact your legacy now and influence generations to come. Counting yourself out is never to be taken lightly. That's why it's so important to NOT COUNT YOURSELF OUT.

As a woman, you experience different emotions for different reasons. There are studies which show that women think differently. I think that is okay. After all, women are made differently. However, it's important to understand your thoughts and take actions as needed to change quickly. Your thoughts lead to actions which, bit by bit, form your life patterns. Do you see how you can count yourself out without even realizing it?

I remember seeing opportunities and not even being willing to apply. Why? I thought there was no way I could be considered. I thought I wasn't worthy or would get a NO. Now, I know that getting a NO isn't easy to accept. However, when you've already decided that there's no way you can get a YES, that's a big problem that needs to be addressed.

At the time of writing this chapter, I received a speaking opportunity with one of the giant companies in a particular industry. I remember seeing the email and closing it quickly (AGAIN, as times past). I thought it could never be me. I wasn't thinking they could actually want me to represent them. I had already counted myself out.

Stop counting yourself out, my friend.

WHY YOU SHOULD STOP COUNTING YOURSELF OUT

When you count yourself out, it impacts not only yourself but also the lives of others and, of course, the world at large. The world is never the same when you count yourself out. You don't pursue opportunities that are life changing to others. You don't implement ideas that have great value. The list is endless and the lost impact is even more devastating.

As a mom of twins, there are so many times I thought I couldn't be a worthy mom. I fell short in so many ways. I had a checklist and I often failed at ticking off the items. That led to some very overwhelming moments as my babies grew. I had unfortunately succumbed to an ideal mom list that was based not on my family's dynamics, which is a major factor in determining what will be best for you family. I had to step back from that list and realize that what's most important is creating a blessed life for my littles, customized based on our family dynamics and needs. You should stop ALREADY counting yourself out based on what you may be thinking are ideal requirements or even shortfalls that you have. Become comfortable with your own self. Your imperfections, failures, and weaknesses all serve to teach you lessons or set the foundation for any improvements or increased learning you may want to pursue.

I started to be okay with who I was – not saying I wouldn't find ways to keep improving as an individual… that's different. For example, to say you couldn't be a speaker since you're too "fat" is selling yourself so short. You have great experiences and lessons to share with others which are in no way impacted by your body size. Don't say you don't have enough low experiences or moments to share with others to encourage them – all our experiences are able to impact others in a powerful way. Be innovative and find different ways to keep going. You may be scared to speak in front of an audience, but you can prerecord videos to share or even write various forms of publications to share with others. In that way, you are still sharing your value and NOT COUNTING YOURSELF OUT!

Be grateful for where you are in life and the lessons learned so far. This changes your trajectory in so many ways. My mom taught me the importance of always finding something to be thankful for! It's the right time NOW to stop selling yourself short, to no longer limit yourself, and to realize that there are so many new areas you can explore – or even revisit areas you aborted. Take a moment to just imagine how your life would be different if you embraced each opportunity without fear or discounting yourself. What does that look like for you? Are you getting excited? Are you ready to take those bold steps? I'm excited for you!

ACTION STEPS

1. Have a real conversation with yourself – in what areas of your life are you counting yourself out?
2. What reasons are leading to you counting yourself out?
3. What changes can you make to stop counting yourself out? Change is necessary to grow.
4. What support will you need to stop counting yourself out?
5. TAKE ACTION ASAP.

Remember to reach out to let me know the life-changing moments you experience when you stop counting yourself out!

He who began a good work in you will see it to completion – Philippians 1:6 NIV

GIRL, DON'T COUNT YOURSELF OUT!

ABOUT KIRSHA

Kirsha Campbell is a CPA/CMA who integrates all the moving parts in your business to set up the right foundation to be recession-proof, operate with reduced risk, increase cashflow, set up effective systems and procedures, and so much more. Kirsha helps business owners say goodbye to being overwhelmed, stressed, and frustrated about their businesses results and operations.

Kirsha values continuous improvement and is sought after for her attention to detail, integrity, and passion for turning businesses around. Having spent years in the corporate world, she understands key strategies that must be adhered to in order to ensure businesses are successful and recession-proof. She also understands the need for businesses to have customized strategies that fit their particular situations. Kirsha is a contributor to Entrepreneur Magazine and has been featured on Thrive Global, Authority Magazine, and American Express for her insights and experiences.

CONNECT WITH KIRSHA

thecashlab.ca

Facebook @kirsha.campbell

LinkedIn @thekirshacampbell

My Life Forever Changed
Julianna Ruggiero, Writer & Advocate

———

THIS IS ABOUT THE DAY THAT CHANGED MY LIFE FOREVER. My dad, Louis P. Ruggiero Jr., could make you laugh, cry, and was a true family man. He truly would give you the shirt off his back – a man with many friends, zero enemies. I guess God needed an angel, so he chose my dad, truly "a one in a million man." In fact, his headstone says, "One in A Million." My life has not been the same since his tragic death and our family is now missing a big piece of our puzzle.

My faith was truly tested on December 15, 2018. It started out as a night of gathering with family and friends at a diner in Fairfield, CT, not realizing this would truly be our last true meal together... forever. We sat at the table laughing, joking, and reminiscing about the good old days. When it came time to say our goodbyes, my dad excused himself to go to the restroom. We realized he was taking longer than normal, so my mom and I went to get the car and waited for him to come out. My dad finally made his way to the car and my mom asked him if everything was okay. My dad being my dad, he said, "Yes, everything's fine." As we approached his sister's house, we all realized my dad hadn't come into the house. My mom walked outside and saw my dad struggling to walk up a small incline in the driveway. When he finally got into the house, he immediately sat in a recliner chair, pale, his hand on his chest. My mom said, "What's the matter?" My dad replied, "I have pain in my chest and back." While quizzing him about his pain, he told us he already took three nitro pills, realizing his doctor always told him, "If you take three nitros and the pain doesn't stop, you need to get to the ER ASAP." So, off my parents went to the hospital, which is literally 5 minutes away.

Because my dad came in with chest pain, he was considered a priority and they began taking his vitals and blood gases right away. For those who don't know, blood gases are extracted by a syringe and sent to the lab to test for any heart damage and a possible heart attack. This test has to be done three times in a time-sensitive manner to confirm accurate results of possible heart damage or heart attack. My dad's first round of results confirmed a heart attack.

The next morning, more tests were done to find out what kind of damage was done to my dad's body. After everything was said and done, the results showed two arteries in his neck were blocked – one was 70% blocked and the other was 100% blocked. Doctors told us that they could fix the artery that was blocked, but they would have to open up his neck. We agreed to have them clean it up. A few days later the surgical consent papers were signed and the surgery was done successfully.

We thought we were out of the woods; everything was fixed and my dad would be released to come home soon. Unfortunately, on December 25, 2018, his heart wasn't working right. Doctors suggested we do open heart surgery on him to try and fix it. We were all hesitant at first because of his history, but we were reassured that this was the next best option for my dad. The surgery was scheduled for that following Monday.

It was Christmas Day and we were hours away from my dad's surgery day. My uncle also happened to be in the same hospital as my dad but they were both on separate floors. We asked a nurse if my dad could come up to my uncle's room so he could spend Christmas day with us and she said yes. That evening, our whole family gathered together in my uncle's hospital room, talking, laughing, and joking around. The nurse only let my dad stay for a few hours, but we made the most of it. Finally, we all went home to get a good night's sleep.

Around 4 am the next morning, I recall waking up randomly out of a dead, sound sleep. My chest was heavy and tears were streaming down my face. Today was the day, the day my dad would get his heart fixed. I kept saying to myself, "Don't worry, today's going to be a hard day, but after this, your father can spend time recovering and he'll be back home." We had to all be at the hospital by 6 am because we wanted to be there to wish my dad luck before he went down to the OR. While we were waiting for the anesthesiologist and operating room nurses to take him down to pre-op, my mom asked me to take a picture with him. Honestly, at first I didn't want to because I didn't look that great and I was tired. Now, looking back, I'm glad we took the picture. I can keep it forever.

We were told by the nurses that two people could go with my dad to be with him in pre-op. At first, we told my aunts to go, but they said they would stay upstairs and wait for me and my mom to come back. So, off we went.

After about 45 minutes or so, my dad got the medicine put through his IV to fall asleep. I remember that he looked calm and content as they were wheeling him away. He smiled and waved to me. The nurses told us not to worry, that they would take good care of him.

I had no idea that would be the last time I would ever see him "normal." That our joy from him making it through such a tough and risky surgery would turn to hell in a matter of days. That I would be a young 19-year-old who lost her father.

One night, a few days after the surgery, we went up to go see my dad. "How are you feeling?" my mom asked him. He couldn't speak due to having an oxygen mask on his face and a tube down his throat. He either had to do sign language, point with his finger, or write on a grease board to talk with us.

He pointed to the area where they did the operation and said in a weak voice, "I'm hurting." His nurse even tried getting him to walk out of his room, with help of course, but he was in a lot of pain and struggled to breathe without the mask.

At dinner time, my dad refused to eat any of the solid food on his dinner tray. He would only drink tiny sips of soup broth. Even with encouragement from the nurse and us, he still refused to eat any of the solid food or try the breathing exercises that he was told to do when a commercial came on TV. I was crying at this point, begging God to make him listen and snap out of it so that he could be one step closer to coming home.

On December 30, 2018, our world turned upside down. My dad had to be sedated again. This time they put him on heavy sedation to make him comfortable. The day before after going down to the "step down" unit, I got a call from my mom saying he had crashed. He was being brought back to the ICU to be intubated.

The cardiologist found pooling around my dad's heart and believed that's why he wasn't waking up. They decided to open him up again and clean up the blood in hopes that it would fix the heart. In addition, they found a pulmonary embolism and kept taking vile after vile of blood every half hour.

On January 1, 2019, New Year's Day, I woke up around 5 am because I couldn't sleep. The ICU nurse was already in the room, giving us the bad news that my dad was getting close to dying. He didn't have much time left and my mom requested a priest to come to his room. So, my family all went into his room and gathered by his bedside, just talking to him and loving on him. I, on the other hand, couldn't make myself go into the room because I knew that if I did, I would lose it. Hearing my family talk to him and cry made me cry. My heart was already breaking due to being the one making the choice to let him go.

It broke even more around 8.35 am. As the priest was reading my dad his last rights, a beam of light shone through the small window of his hospital room. We knew the time was near. The heart monitor indicated my dad had passed away.

My father's death has changed me. I'm not the same person I was before he died: grief stole my will to continue writing and I knew I had to take time to try and pick up the pieces of my life going forward. It's been a struggle, but I'm slowly coming back. Grief and these last three years after this loss has brought forth challenge after challenge and struggle after struggle. I manage the best I can through it all, despite everything I went through during that period.

I do know, in my heart of hearts, my dad would truly want me to move forward in all aspects of my life. I truly believe in the grace of God: He has been my savior through all of this. I am a practicing Catholic and my faith tells me I will see my dad and loved ones again one day. I do believe in life after death.

"Tell someone you love them. Hug them tight because tomorrow is never promised." – Juliana Ruggiero

GIRL, DON'T COUNT YOURSELF OUT!

ABOUT JULIANA

Juliana Ruggiero is a is a writer, columnist, advocate, and author with cerebral palsy. One of her greatest goals in life to become a successful writer. In doing so, she would also love to become a life coach. She has much to offer others going through the same life experiences because, as we all know, everyone has a story that should be told – good, bad, or ugly. When not writing, she can be found helping her mom prep a meal, exercising through bowling, or scouring the internet for the latest and greatest next big gaming app. You can find Juliana's work on various sites such as The Mighty, Herstory, Unwritten, Coffee House Writers, and Project Wednesday (now known as The Plant Room).

CONNECT WITH JULIANA

Facebook @juliana.ruggiero

Discovering Your Hidden Talents

Dr. Daphne Soares, Author & Business Coach

When I got married in my home country, I had a beautiful senior executive job and drew a very good salary. We had dated for nearly six years and knew each other well, inside and out. I was super excited as he was the love of my life and now we could live together, happily ever after.

Unplanned, within less than two months my husband got a job offer in the Gulf. After a lot of prayer and discussion, we decided that he should take this opportunity and accept the offer for the future of our family. Our parents weren't pleased with the idea of him leaving me and going to another country, but they respected our decision.

We decided that I would stay with my parents till I could join him. After he left, I discovered I was with child. I was overjoyed. I would have my very own living doll to play with and cuddle. When I was in my seventh month, we decided that I would quit my job and become a stay home mom so I could prep for the arrival of our firstborn and give her undivided attention.

We were blessed with a cute little princess. My husband applied for leave for her birth but was only able to come down after around two weeks. Thank God for the many good friends and family who came forward to help and support me. Me and my little one received loads of pampering, though I dearly missed my husband's presence. When our little one was eight months old, my husband was able to arrange a home and take us to the Gulf. We were so excited to be reunited and live together again, giving our little one all the love and cuddles she deserved.

In the Gulf, life was very different. I remained a stay home mom – especially as we had no extended family or support and didn't want our princess to be raised by a nanny. When our princess was a year old, I fell pregnant again. We were blessed with a little prince charming. Our family was complete and my hands were full taking care of the home and both kids that were less than two years apart. My husband had long working hours and, in the interest of the kids, we decided that I should take care of them personally. I treasured every moment as I raised the kids myself and saw them grow beautifully.

When they started school, I would feel very lonely despite there being lots of chores to keep me occupied. I missed having human beings around me and someone my age to talk to and share with. My days were spent like any normal mom: picking up and dropping off the kids, teaching them, cleaning, washing, changing bed linens, ironing, and cooking. I seldom went out as we were able to order everything online and get it delivered to the doorstep. Besides, the heat was killer and it was never a good idea to venture outdoors during the summer months. This was my daily routine. Time passed very quickly and by the end of the day I would be dead beat. I could feel myself growing exhausted and burning out. Yet, I would not utter a word and always smile. With this, the gap in my work experience kept increasing.

I wasn't interested in teaching in a school, as I had always worked in the corporate sector and the salaries in education were no good. I volunteered my time freely in the church and taught the faith when the kids would attend catechism classes. This was very convenient, as we all travelled and returned together on weekends. As the kids grew, expenses increased. It was getting a bit tough to manage with one salary, as you can imagine.

I looked high and low for a job with no luck, as I didn't have any local experience. I started lifting this in prayer. I even went on to ask friends if they would refer me. At times, I would sit and cry, knowing I had talent. I started questioning God as to why no one wanted my services. Why weren't they giving me a chance to show off my knowledge and capabilities? The questions went on and on, popping up in my mind.

This was very upsetting, as I had thirteen years of working experience before motherhood in my home country. This was crazy, right? I started brainstorming and looking for ways to work. I didn't think too much about how I would manage all the household chores once I started working, although making sure the kids were never neglected or without any parent there for them was always on our minds. I just trusted the good Lord, asking Him to help make a way.

It didn't happen immediately, but God did show me a way in His time through an announcement that there was an upcoming online psychology course. I jumped at this opportunity. I had no idea where this would lead me, but the thought of online training from the comfort of my home was definitely a treat. I could interact with other people yet be able to care of my family. This led me to doing my master's from the US in the faith. Woohoo! This was exciting. I loved and treasured every new learning experience, but the thought of getting a paid job was still on my mind.

I did my best not to lose hope. I unfolded every opportunity the good Lord offered. I moved on from the online psychology course to complete my master's in the faith and a diploma in psychology. Through these I discovered my hidden talents. This was a new avenue that brought me great joy. Having explored further, I found my way to studying counseling and NLP (Neuro Linguistic Programming). Never had I thought that this was something I would really love and enjoy. Through all this, I was able to understand myself, my husband, my children, and everyone around me better. I was more understanding, more patient, and stopped getting frustrated is trying situations. I had a major shift in mentality and tapped into my inner peace.

This led me to walk even more miles to learning. The hunger grew with each passing day. Still, I didn't know what the Lord had in store for me. As much as all this was good and I felt great, I needed a job. I needed to earn money. I could feel something deep inside aglow and I decided to share my knowledge with other moms. Little did I know that they were victims of so much violence, trauma, disrespect, and burn-out. They needed someone to hear them in a non-judgmental zone. Someone they could trust. They were searching for healing and support. I was able to combine my faith experiences and learnings with psychology and counseling. Before I knew it, the word had spread. More and more women started contacting me with their problems. Many faced issued with their small children, teens, and young adults. I felt great joy when I could uplift these people and give them hope and a new beginning. They were able to overcome many limiting beliefs and fears. This led me to pause and think. Could this become a means of income for me? These people needed my help ,so why not go into offering my services? Friends told me I was crazy if I was thinking of making it my career. I didn't let myself be weighed down by their negative comments. I had a chat with my husband about doing this as a business and he said in surprise, "A business? Do you even know how to run a business and all that is needed? You have lost your mind. Business? No. A job in this area is okay, if you get one." This broke my heart and I went and cried bitterly in silence. It hurt deep inside. Even he did not believe in my capabilities. My only hope was in the Lord; I wasn't going to give up so easily. I decided that I would walk out in faith and I prayed that God let me know His will for our future and the family. I would prove my capabilities by remaining focused and putting my heart and soul into it.

I would spend time listening to these women and all they were going through. I started training them in building their self-confidence and overcoming emotional blocks and trauma. I did not stop learning there but decided to keep enriching my knowledge, so I could stay up to date with the times and give my best to all who needed me. I moved on to doing another in-depth NLP certification from Australia. From there I took a leap of faith to moving on to a coaching certification, again from Australia and the UAE. Now I had more tools in my Mary Poppins bag. I felt excited about the path that lay in front of me and I just had to trust the good Lord and myself. I walked in faith, without losing focus or hope. I would spend time in silence and contemplation.

I decided not to limit myself only to my country, seeing the demand from all sides. As faith would have it, I started getting people from Africa, Italy, the USA, Australia, the UK, Canada, Bangladesh, New Zealand, Jordan, and many more countries reaching out to me for help. This is how Carousel Moms Business and Leadership Coaching was born. The name, logo, and brand colors are the creation of our gorgeous daughter – my son helps with other office work while my husband started contributing to helping around the home. I feel so blessed and rewarded for all the love and time invested in them. Finally, my husband said, "Wow. I am so proud of you. You are a super woman."

I have received many international awards and recognition for my services globally. I have also been featured in international magazines and channels. Nothing is impossible if we only believe in ourselves and walk in faith, without losing our purpose in life. If you've read this far, congratulations. Believe in yourself. If I can do it, so can you. Yes, we're all different and have various talents. Use your talents wisely, for the glory of God, and to help your neighbor. People need you and are looking out for your help. Learn to be an instrument for the Lord and serve others around you.

We women have so much potential and can do so much. We need to be a source of inspiration for our children. Do not let ourselves be abused, tortured, and sit and cry. We are created for something much greater. How do you expect your child to learn and want to learn if they don't have a role model to follow? There is no one better than you to inspire them. Who said that we moms were only meant to take care of the home and do the chores? After all, a home is built by both parents. Children need good role models. It's important that we get our partners involved in the home. Now I live life on my own terms, living my dreams. I'm still able to care for the home, the kids, and my family. I don't work a day because I believe that when you do what you love and are passionate about, you never truly work.

Always keep the faith strong in yourself and in God. Nurture your faith by reading God's word daily and spending quality time in silence, so you may hear God speak to your heart. With God's support, you will not be shaken and will stand strong when the storms of life hit.

GIRL, DON'T COUNT YOURSELF OUT!

ABOUT DR. DAPHNE

Dr. Daphne Soares is the founder and CEO of Carousel Moms Business and Leadership Coaching. She has been ranked #7 among the Top 30 Business Coaches for 2022 by The NYC Journal, Top Women Leaders in 2022 by Passion Vista, and Top 10 Female Coaches in 2021 by Yahoo Finance. Awardee of numerous international awards and recognitions, she is the Amazon #1 bestselling author of Don't Judge a Book by Its Cover, Business Success, Embracing Imperfections 2, and Created for Greatness with the global legend Les Brown, to name a few.

Dr. Daphne is a certified business and leadership coach, author, international speaker, and mentor. She has gone from a 9-5 job to homemaker, confirmation coordinator, masters' catechist, counsellor, hypnotherapist, psychotherapist, and timeline therapist. She is passionate about empowering women globally to create thriving businesses, build self-confidence, overcome limiting beliefs, and set healthy boundaries at home and in the workplace.

CONNECT WITH DR. DAPHNE

linktr.ee/carouselmoms

Facebook @carouselmoms

OH NO, YOU'RE NOT DOCTOR...
I NEED MY FOOT!
STAR HOLMES-WORD, AUTHOR &
CONFIDENCE COACH

MY DAY STARTED OUT NORMALLY: I WAS PREPARING TO TAKE my shower. I turned on some music to create a vibe that helps me transcend to a place that feels inspirational. Music is an integral part of my life – when I feel down, it lifts me up; when I need to clear my thoughts, it takes me deep into the rhythm and heartbeat of the melody.

By the time I finished taking my shower, I wrapped myself in my favorite turquoise towel with bold white stripes and tucked the corner of it on the inside, to hold my towel snug. I sat on the bed in preparation of slathering on cocoa butter.

Today was different. I lifted my left leg up to lay it across to my right leg. I glanced down at my left foot and immediately noticed that my big toe on my left foot was black. I was nervous to touch it, but I knew I needed to. It felt hard to the touch.

My emotions were instantly stirring inside of my body. My level of concern went from zero to one hundred (and real quick). I had previous medical training and experience as a medical assistant. I therefore knew what it meant when I saw my toe: it was either dead or dying. In short, it hadn't been receiving the proper circulation. To be honest, in that moment I wanted to act like I didn't know how bad things were.

Panic started to creep in, so I took a deep breath and regained my composure as best I could under the circumstances.

I moved swiftly (limping in pain) down the stairs to tell my sister what was happening and inform her that I needed to go to the emergency room.

I could tell it freaked her out when I removed my sock and she saw my foot. My sister said, "Yes, I do think you need to go to the emergency room." I asked her to take a picture of my toe as I picked up my cell phone to call one of my brothers, who was upstairs in his room. I asked him to take me to the ER due to foot issues and he agreed.

My foot was in a lot of pain. I was incredibly nervous, even though I tried not to show how nervous I was. My sister knows me well (she says I'm theatrical) so she usually doesn't believe me when I tell her that I'm in a lot of pain. My tolerance is much lower than hers. But this time, she seemed to believe me. She had a look of concern on her face.

You may be wondering, when did this all begin? Well, I was diagnosed with type 2 diabetes in 2010.

When the doctor diagnosed me, it just didn't seem to register that I had a chronic disease – a disease that would drastically change how my body would respond to everything I put in it. That I could die if I didn't take care of myself.

I was told by my doctor that I had gestational diabetes when pregnant with my children, a condition where blood sugar levels become high during pregnancy (WebMD). There are two types of gestational diabetes. The first is controlled by diet and exercise, the second by insulin.

After I had both of my oldest children, I was diagnosed with the type 2 insulin dependent diabetes. Injecting myself with insulin had become a required part of my daily life. At first I didn't feel sick, so there were times when I wouldn't take the insulin. I was living life and moving towards my goals and dreams A diabetes education regimen wasn't on my mind most days.

When I opened my first business, Easy Street Ultra Lounge (a sleek New York style ultra-lounge in Cedar Rapids, Iowa), I would go to work most days without taking any meds.

It seemed to catch up to me, though, because when I got pregnant with my third child, I was sick. The in-bed-all-day kind of sick. There was no energy in my body and it seemed to make me feel like I was alien green all the time.

To help me feel better (I was desperate), I started taking my medication on a regular routine.

After the birth of my third child, I got home and felt like a new woman! I recall going outside a day or so after getting home with the baby and twirling in the grass as I stared at the beautiful blue sky, with clouds as whites as marshmallows. I felt like a child: full of bliss and happiness.

The bliss fizzled out once I remembered that, while I was pregnant with baby number three, we'd had to close the event lounge because of financial reasons. In addition to closing the ultra-lounge, my husband expressed a desire to go back home to Tennessee.

He came to Iowa to get married in 2008. I felt like, since he came to Iowa to marry me, I would be agreeable to going to live nearer to his family, so that the baby could experience growing up near the family my husband so dearly loved. In 2014 we moved to TN.

For the next several years my inner entrepreneur lay dormant. During that time I worked a nine to five, staffing for client care.

One of the most problematic parts about working in that office was dealing with the personalities of unhappy women.

My health continued to decline. I still wasn't taking my meds as consistently as needed and ended up in the hospital with a second case of walking pneumonia.

When I was well enough to go home, I took better care of myself. I was scared about struggling to breathe and feeling so ill.

I started to realize that a couple of things were inhibiting me from focusing on taking better care of myself. Personal family matters had weighed on me heavily. When I was stressed, I would forget to take my medications.

Being a fervent woman that believes in God helped me become determined to win this health crisis.

I still had a couple of things that could impede me from winning. One was smoking cigarettes, the other was taking my meds daily.

While at my desk, I was listening to a random radio station on the internet and heard about an upcoming woman's conference being held in Dallas.

The feeling that came over me when I heard about this conference was like God was telling me I needed to be there!

I made it to the conference and it was an amazing experience. There was so many beautiful, brown-complected women – and every shade in between – all in the same place at the same time, talking, teaching, and sharing positive energy.

All for the purpose of growing personally and professionally on their entrepreneurial journeys.

This was the first time I'd experienced women in such a sizeable magnitude, sharing their successes and deficiencies in business.

The conference changed me. It inspired me to reach higher!

I could see how God had designed my life to be different than what my childhood trauma presented to me daily.

I instantly understood why I'd received all the jobs and training that I had. They were to prepare me to work with women all over the world. What a revelation that was.

When I got home from that conference, I started putting together an overall plan for how I was going to implement all that uniqueness I'd learned.

Connecting with other entrepreneurs on the Internet and networking became a normal, daily inspiration for me. I began using social media often, despite the initial nervous feelings that made my knees shake the first time I went "live" on Facebook.

I wanted to share my new world of learning, growing, and scaling your business to the next level with people that were in my circle of influence.

I went on, overtly learning from other coaches. I enrolled in several coaching programs during this time.

Something that I discovered early on is how learning and growing coincide in the arena of coaching, speaking, and writing when you're working to establish yourself as credible.

To begin building my credibility, I started with compiling my first book: an anthology written with eleven other women.

I served as an ambassador for several conferences and summits where I was blessed to connect with even more creative, brilliant women.

Requests started coming in for interviews on podcasts and live Internet shows.

I was in the planning stages of compiling my second book anthology when, suddenly, we were hit with the pandemic.

Everything paused. My book project was placed on hold, my health declined, my bank account declined, and my appearances on social media were almost null and void. My marriage was going through a rough patch and I'd decided to move to Atlanta.

The move to Atlanta was important to me. I wasn't raised with all my siblings, so I jumped at the chance to live with a few of them and be nearer to my mother. Mom had retired and moved to Atlanta.

Let's get back to me going to the emergency room.

The plethora of standard operating procedures were carried out and I was informed that they were indeed admitting me. I stayed in the hospital for four days.

During my hospitalization, the doctors and surgeons went back and forth deciding whether they should amputate my big toe.

A procedure was done – they placed two stints in my left leg to increase circulation. The procedure worked and I was able to get out of the hospital under the care of my new podiatrist. They did not amputate my toe!

Being admitted to the hospital this time was like pushing a re-set button.

I stopped smoking cigarettes and was reeducated on how to take my meds so that they would provide me with the most sustainable, healthy outcome. My husband visited every day and we watched movies and played cards.

My sister, my niece, and I were able to fly to Dallas to attend the business conference that started it all.

I got back on social media, started rebranding myself, and began working on my next three book projects! I focus on my health daily. I have a medication schedule that I follow rigorously and I take my supplements and exercise. I'm feeling better than I have in years.

I remind myself often that I have unrestricted access to God. He placed inside of us everything that we need to be successful and confident.

I needed to remember to dig deep, do the work to heal, and pray often.

"Focus on making yourself better, not thinking you are." Unknown

GIRL, DON'T COUNT YOURSELF OUT!

ABOUT STAR

Star M. Holmes-Word is an author, speaker, and coach. She has spent over ten years helping women find their most confident selves as a domestic violence and sexual assault advocate. Star was trained through the Coalition for Domestic Violence and Sexual Assault.

Star began her speaking career during her tenure at Waypoint Services as DV/SA and multicultural outreach advocate. She pivoted to coaching, speaking, and writing in 2017, at which point speaking opportunities for internet interviews, blog radio shows, women's conferences, and in-person education sessions increased.

Star compiled her first anthology in 2018, titled We Are Women of Substance Vol 1. She is currently organizing Vol 2 and Vol 3.

Star targeted her niche and selected key components of domestic violence training to create her signature coaching program for leaders to learn how to live their best, most confident lives.

CONNECT WITH STAR

starholmesword.com

Facebook and Instagram @yorastartoo

CANCER TOUCHED DOWN
BELINDA SALLEY, MPA & CONSULTANT

BEFORE I SHARE MY UNWANTED ENTANGLEMENT WITH STAGE three breast cancer, let me give you some insight into how my life was evolving. I'm the proud mother of two beautiful, talented daughters. Darnajah is a twenty year old working full time and trying to find her footing in life. Dasia is sixteen, a junior in high school, bestselling author and an athlete.

Raising two girls can be chaotic — being taxi, ATM, chef, chaperone, and often referee between **THE GIRLS**. In addition to making sure they're thriving, I'm a full-time social worker and business owner. While living in the moment managing my business, producing content, and nine to five, your girl needed a staycation.

While I was enjoying the hustle and grind of packing merchandise, post office runs, and sporting events, I was burnt out and ready for a girl's trip. **My confirmation** came upon arriving home from work and receiving a call from Dasia asking, "Can you CashApp me a few dollars? My friends and I want to get food." I just sighed and sent the money.

Not more than ten minutes passed and Darmajah called to complain that Dasia wore her jeans that she told her not to wear.

STAYCATION

"Lord, have mercy," I responded, "I'll talk to Dasia." Well that was enough for me. I called my bestie and told her we need a getaway to Atlantic City. With the Covid-19 pandemic, work, the girls, and mental overload — rest and relaxation is what the doctor would recommend. She asked, "When do you want to go?" I said, "Let' try for the third weekend in September."

The girl's trip is on, let the good times roll. The girls were situated and I was ready to hit the road. You know the saying, **"What happens in Atlantic City stays in AC"**. We packed our Moscato, snacks, and music. Once we got settled in our room, it was time to enjoy our view and put on some music before we headed to the casino.

After we lost our money in the casino we went to dinner. Upon returning to the room the party continued with dancing and shots. The car ride had us tired, so we prepared for bed. As I was taking my shower, I felt a lump. It caught me off guard because I didn't remember feeling it earlier. Anyway, I wasn't going to let it ruin my vacation. I had convinced myself it was a cyst and I'd just keep checking it.

PRAYER TIME

The next morning I felt the lump and got scared. The texture changed and it seemed to be larger. I told my bestie to feel it and she responded "What is that?" I replied, "I would love to know." She said "Make sure you call the doctor and have it checked when you get home." We got our day started — first the pool then back to the room to change for dinner and more gambling. Our vacation seemed to be coming to an end in the blink of an eye. Check out time drew near and reality started to set in. One thing was for sure — we had a great weekend and it was needed.

I took my mind off the lump until my bestie reminded me. When I'm faced with uncertainty, I always go to **God** in prayer. I called the doctor the next day and made my appointment. After I called my mom, who's my rock, to share with her about the lump. She told me not to worry and asked if she needed to come with me to my appointment. My appointment was two months away due to the pandemic. Knowing it was six weeks, I started to get nervous because of the unknown.

Finally, the time came to get my mammogram and talk with the doctor. After my exam the doctor informed me that my results would be mailed in two weeks. I paused, "That seems like an eternity to wait." He reminded me that I have dense breast tissue and had a cyst in the past. Hearing the doctor explain that made me feel a little **SENSE** of relief.

TRUSTING THE PROCESS / TRANSPARENCY

A couple of weeks later, I was folding clothes and **REALIZED** that I didn't get my results. After talking to my bestie, she suggested I call the doctor. Two days before Thanksgiving, my gynecologist called and asked me to come in the next day because she had my results. I couldn't sleep, wondering why my doctor wanted me to come in as opposed to mailing me my results. The next morning, I was leaving for my appointment and the nerves were getting to me. The doctor called me in the back and asked if there was someone I could call to share my results with. I said, "You can call my mom."

She called my mom and disclosed that my results showed breast cancer in the left breast. I immediately begin to cry. The doctor proceeds to ask me whether I was Christian. I replied, "Yes." She prayed for me and told me to hold on to my faith and everything would be okay. She told me I could stay in the room if I needed and gave me recommendations for two doctors and asked which one I would prefer?

I **CHOSE** the male oncologist because he had been practicing longer and the hospital was close. The doctor called and scheduled my first appointment and told me to call her if I had any questions. My mind was racing and I just started praying, "Lord, you're able to do all things; through Your stripes I'm healed; The Lord is my Shepherd." I just kept repeating all these scriptures to help me calm down in order to drive home. I finally got myself together to drive home and relax before the girls got home. I didn't want the girls to see me crying.

SHOCKING TREATMENT PLAN

Reality set in — I have breast cancer and it was time to meet my oncologist. My friend went with me to the doctor. He asked a lot of questions about my family history before examining me. He reviewed my MRI and told me he needed to see my last five years of mammograms. He wanted to do another ultrasound and requested that I do genetic testing to see if I inherited the BRCA gene which is a gene in your DNA that increases the risk of breast cancer.

The doctor reassured me that all my tests would be reviewed with his team before we moved forward. He also stated that I could ask the nurse navigator any questions I had. I called and requested my five years of mammograms and was told to pick them up in two days. My next visit was more intense because I found out it was **Stage 2** and because of the size I would have to get a mastectomy as opposed to the lumpectomy. I had no more tears to cry. I just wanted to get the surgery over with because the mass was growing.

In preparation of my surgery date, March 10, 2020, the nurse told me to get the leave papers from my job so she could fill them out. I told the girls that I would be having surgery and either they were strong or they didn't process it at that moment. Life went on as usually and I made up in my mind that it had to be done because my breast was **literally** killing me.

I had been praying every day for strength to get through it and I heard God say, "You need to share your journey." Until now, I had only told a few family members and friends. **HOWEVER**, every day God kept saying, "Share your journey." I finally said, "Okay God, I will use my social media to tell my story." From that day I shared the good, bad, and ugly of cancer.

I asked if I needed chemotherapy and radiation. However, my nurse didn't want me to focus on the after treatment. Once everything was finalized, she told me to go see Dr. Cooperman who would be the plastic surgeon. "Why do I need a plastic surgeon?" The nurse told me I will have an expander placed in my breast after the surgery and suggested that I have a conversation with the plastic surgeon.

FIGHTING MY BEST FIGHT

I called my mom with the surgery date and she said, "I'll be there a few days before." That made me feel good, knowing she would take good care of me. While getting mentally prepared for the surgery, I continued doing my daily routine and incorporated several doctors' appointments. I had to do MRIs, blood work, COVID tests, and paperwork in preparation for my sick leave.

Time flies. The big day had arrived and as we got closer to the hospital, my nerves got to me but put my game face on. I had pre-registered so all I had to do was sign in and find out where to go. We made it upstairs and were greeted by the nurse in charge. I changed into my gown and went live on social media to ask my tribe for prayers. My mom prayed with me then I went off to surgery. When I woke up my mouth was dry and my roommate was yelling loud for pain medication. I wanted to feel my breast but decided against it.

About twenty minutes later some doctors came in stating they were the ones assisting my doctors with my surgery. They had come to see how I was feeling and to check my incision. The doctor asked me if I wanted to see it but, at that time, I wasn't ready. I was told I would get pain medication every four hours and that my surgeons would be in to see me later.

ADAPTING TO MY NEW NORMAL

While in the hospital I had some difficult nights when the pain medication wore off. However, when it was time for discharge, I was so happy to see my mom and get out of that hospital. I signed all the papers and waited for my wheelchair. When I arrived home the girls were so happy to see me and my phone was ringing off the hook. My mom got me home and settled then went back out to get my medication. I don't remember much of those first two days home because the **Percocet** had me asleep for most of it.

The third day I refused to take them and just took Tylenol instead. I was able to get out of bed and recline in the living room. What happened a few hours later was nothing but love, flowers, food, and gift bags pouring in for me. I started crying and thanking God for my amazing tribe. I shared my progress on social media not realizing how many people I had been **touching**. The feedback, calls, and texts were all about how **courageous** I had been. I felt pretty good except for my three drains which I named my power packs. My drains had to be cleaned every three hours and that was the hardest part.

Two weeks later, I went to see my plastic surgeon and he took my drains out. That pain was something fierce but I was so happy to have the drains removed. I started a Facebook live stream and everyone was so happy to see me. I stayed on the live stream until Facebook ended the live. A few minutes after that, I was delighted to be visited by my three besties who showed up with my favorite seafood. We ate and I had a chance to talk about my new normal without breasts. I thank God for walking with and through this battle with me.

CANCER PICKED THE WRONG CHICK

My new journey encompassed sixteen weeks of chemotherapy every Monday for four hours of infusions. I won't bore you with all the details, just know it was long and I was fatigued and nauseated after every treatment. However, I didn't miss an appointment or reschedule due to complications. The most important takeaway from this is having an amazing team of doctors who care. On my last day of treatment my bestie went with me for support as I ran the bell.

Chemotherapy recovery time was two weeks then I prepared for my next battle — radiation. Once **AGAIN,** more treatment; this time every day for thirty days. I just wanted it to be over so I could move on with my life. The first two weeks were a breeze. The third week, I was literally on fire and my neck and breast had third degree burns. I had to ask God to give me strength. My doctor wanted me to take Percocet, but I refused and was given 800mg of Tylenol and a burn cream called Silver Sulfadiazine instead.

I was taking medication but still had no relief. With six days left, I wanted to quit but I knew my life depended on this treatment to kill any cancer cells that metastasized to another area of the breast. When the last day finally came the team was in the front waiting for me. I was exhausted and tried to get out of doing the last treatment but knew that wasn't going to happen so I said to myself "only the strong survive." I got through it and was ready to ring the bell. My entire team came. I read my declaration and rang that bell so hard. The tears started rolling — I'm **CANCER FREE!** Now I am working to lower the age of mammograms to thirty-five and speaking to the masses on breast cancer awareness.

"Life threw me lemons and I made a gallon of lemonade trusting my God." - Belinda Salley

GIRL, DON'T COUNT YOURSELF OUT!

ABOUT BELINDA

Motivational speaker Belinda Salley was born on May19, 1968, in Newark, New Jersey. She's the mother of two beautiful daughters, Darnajah Edmond (twenty) and Dasia Edmond (seventeen years old). She graduated from Frank H. Morrell High School in Irvington, New Jersey. She obtained her bachelor's degree in early childhood education from Montclair State University and joined the Finer Women of Zeta Phi Beta Sorority Incorporated. After graduating, she secured a job at Essex County Division of Welfare in March of 1994 as a family service worker. While working, Salley continued her education at Rutgers University in Newark, New Jersey where she graduated in 2014.

She received her master's degree in Public Administration in 2020. Salley is also an active member in The Order of Eastern Star. Salley was diagnosed with stage three invasive lobular carcinoma breast cancer and went from depression to designer when she created a sneaker and clothing line to challenge others to "BCourageous."

CONNECT WITH BELINDA

Business: Facebook.com/BCourageousLLC

Personal: Facebook.com/belinda.salley

Instagram @bcourageous_

What's Next?

Step into becoming the most empowered and uplifted version of yourself. Step out of your comfort zone and into your power!

Girl, Don't Count Yourself Out! – Volume 2 Coming January 2023

Stay connected with the "Girl, Don't Count Yourself Out" Community on Facebook and Instagram for ongoing inspiration and more details.

https://www.facebook.com/GirlDontCountYourselfOut

https://www.instagram.com/girldontcountyourselfout/

Made in the USA
Middletown, DE
01 October 2023

39476295R00066